OHIO WILDLIFE VIEWING GUIDE

W. H. (CHIP) GROSS, AUTHOR AND PROJECT MANAGER

ILLUSTRATIONS BY JOHN A. RUTHVEN

FALCON

Falcon Press® Publishing Co., Inc.,
Helena, Montana

ACKNOWLEDGMENTS

The *Ohio Wildlife Viewing Guide* was made possible by the Ohio Division of Wildlife. Special thanks are due the following organizations and their representatives who participated on the Ohio Watchable Wildlife Steering Committee:

American Electric Power - James McWilliams
American Fisheries Society - Perry Orndorff
Ducks Unlimited - Larry Harmon
League of Ohio Sportsmen - Steve Stechshulte
Mead Corporation - Walt Smith
National Audubon Society - Steve Sedam
National Rifle Association - Philip Gray
National Wild Turkey Federation - Walt Ingram
Ohio B.A.S.S. Chapter Federation, Inc. - Dennis Becker
Ohio Bowhunters Association - Steve Meeks
Ohio Conservation Coalition - Dean Hinebaugh
Ohio Department of Transportation - Debbie Brown
Ohio Fish and Wildlife Management Association - Gildo Tori
Ohio Game Protectors Association - Jim Abrams
Ohio Huskie Muskie Club - Max Case
Ohio Lepidopterists - Eric Metzler
Ohio Sport Fishing Federation - Mark Spisak
Ohio State Trappers Association - Doug Haubert
Ohio Wildlife Federation - Steve Stechshulte
Ohio Wildlife Rehabilitators Association - Betty Ross
Pheasants Forever - John Beall
Ruffed Grouse Society - Dan Dozer
The Wildlife Society - Lynda Andrews
U.S. Forest Service - Lynda Andrews

Last, but certainly not least, we thank internationally renowned Ohio wildlife artist John A. Ruthven for his excellent opaque-watercolor paintings illustrating this book. His renderings of 36 Ohio wildlife species feature those mammals, birds, reptiles, amphibians, fishes, and insects most representative of the six ecological regions of our state.

Author:
W. H. (Chip) Gross

Illustrations:
John A. Ruthven

Front Cover Photo:
Northern Cardinal by Jim Roetzel

Back Cover Photos:
Red Fox by Ron Austing
White-tailed Deer by Jim Roetzel

TABLE OF CONTENTS

WILDLIFE VIEWING DISTRICT FOUR (SOUTHEAST OHIO)

WILDLIFE VIEWING DISTRICT FIVE (SOUTHWEST OHIO)

Design, typesetting, and other prepress work by Falcon Press, Helena,
Montana.

Printed in Korea

ISBN 1-56044-491-6

Library of Congress Cataloging-in-Publication Data
    Gross, W. H. (Warren H.), 1951-
        Ohio wildlife viewing guide / W.H. "Chip" Gross.
                p.   cm.
        ISBN 1-56044-491-6 (pbk.)
        1. Wildlife viewing sites--Ohio--Guidebooks. 2. Wildlife
    watching--Ohio--Guidebooks. 3. Ohio--Guidebooks. I. Title.
    QL198.G76 1996
    333.78'09771--dc20   96-16409
                                                              CIP

PROJECT SPONSORS

 The OHIO DIVISION OF WILDLIFE is the state agency responsible for the management of Ohio's fish and wildlife resources, and operates under a broad set of authorities found in the Ohio Revised Code. For more information, contact the Ohio Division of Wildlife, 1840 Belcher Drive, Columbus, OH 43224-1329, or telephone 1-800-WILDLIFE or 614-265-6300. Mission statement: *We are dedicated to conserving and improving the fish and wildlife resources and their habitats, and promoting their use and appreciation by the public so that these resources continue to enhance the quality of life for all Ohioans.*

 DEFENDERS OF WILDLIFE is a nonprofit organization of more than 100,000 members and supporters dedicated to preserving the natural abundance and diversity of wildlife and its habitat. A 1-year membership is $20 and includes a subscription to *Defenders,* an award-winning conservation magazine. To join, or for further information, write or call Defenders of Wildlife, 1101 14th Street NW, Suite 1400, Washington, D.C. 20005; (202) 682-9400.

 DEPARTMENT OF DEFENSE (DOD) is the steward of about 25 million acres of land in the United States, many of which possess irreplaceable natural and cultural resources. The DOD is pleased to support the Watchable Wildlife Program through its Legacy Resource Management Program, a special initiative to enhance the conservation and restoration of natural and cultural resources on military land. For more information contact the Office of the Deputy Under Secretary of Defense (Environmental Security), 400 Navy Drive, Suite 206, Arlington, VA 22202-2884.

INTRODUCTION

Welcome to the *Ohio Wildlife Viewing Guide!*

During the summer and fall of 1995, I had the privilege of visiting approximately 140 of the best wildlife viewing sites in Ohio. The 80 sites in this guide (selected by the Ohio Watchable Wildlife Steering Committee, listed on the Acknowledgments page) are the best of those sites—the best of the best.

I began my statewide tour in the 95-degree heat and humidity of July and ended with the first snowflakes of November. I drove thousands of miles, spent hundreds of hours, walked miles of trails, and had a great time. I was pleasantly surprised to find that, at many sites, especially during weekdays, I had the area or trail entirely to myself. My hope is that you will enjoy these wildlife viewing sites as much as I did.

When you visit, take a good pair of binoculars or a spotting scope, a field guide, a camera . . . and your time. Don't rush. Plan to visit only one or two areas per day so that you can gear down to the slower pace of the natural world. You'll enjoy each site more, and you'll see more wildlife.

Try visiting the same site in different seasons, too. A new season brings migratory wildlife and triggers behavioral changes in resident creatures. No area is ever the same twice.

While exploring wild sites, I also encountered a highly urban, industrial, and agricultural Buckeye State. Yet, among cities, factories, and farmlands, small glimpses of wild Ohio—the Ohio that was—remain. Vast marshes, windy prairies, silent forests, and the wild creatures and wild plants they sustain, are still there.

These wild areas reveal not only Ohio's past, but its future as well. They are critical wildlife habitats that deserve our protection. As human populations increase, so does the value of such areas—for wildlife and for us.

In his famous book, *A Sand County Almanac,* Aldo Leopold wrote, "There are some who can live without wild things, and some who cannot." I cannot, and it is my guess that you cannot, either. May no future generation of those "who cannot" have reason to say that, because of us, no wild things or wild places remain.

W.H. (Chip) Gross
Author and Project Manager
January 1996

DO SOMETHING WILD!

Share Your Tax Refund With Wildlife.

The success of Ohio's endangered species and wildlife diversity program depends on **YOU**! Your financial support has allowed the Division of Wildlife to acquire and restore critical habitat, to research lesser known species of wildlife, to reintroduce and reestablish various species to their native Ohio habitats, and to educate children and adults on the subjects of wildlife diversity and endangered species.

On the Ohio State Income Tax Form, there is a line where you can designate that a portion or all of your income tax refund be donated to the Ohio Division of Wildlife's Endangered Species and Wildlife Diversity Fund. By marking the appropriate box and filling in a dollar amount, you've made your contribution! That's all it takes—no checks or additional stamps, envelopes, or trips to the post office.

If you aren't due a tax refund, you can still help; and your donation is deductible on next year's income tax return. Simply send a check to:

> Endangered Wildlife Special Account
> Ohio Division of Wildlife
> 1840 Belcher Drive
> Columbus, Ohio 43224-1329

And what exactly does your money do for endangered species and wildlife diversity in Ohio? It helps the Division of Wildlife buy and/or restore land and water that will provide a home to many species of wildlife. With this funding, the Division has purchased 1,481 acres of wetlands—habitat utilized by 60 percent of the wildlife species on Ohio's endangered species list.

Income tax checkoff money has been used to fund research projects enabling the Division of Wildlife to learn more about managing Ohio's endangered species and wildlife diversity. Using income tax checkoff dollars, efforts are underway to reestablish populations of paddlefish, river otters, lake sturgeon, and other endangered or threatened species.

The income tax checkoff also provides funds for many educational efforts, including Project WILD, a hands-on program that offers Ohio's youth a close look at the natural world, and WILD School Sites, a program that establishes actual wildlife habitats/learning labs on school grounds. Wildlife Diversity Grants have been awarded to researchers and educators. Grant recipients have established aquatic labs at schools, introduced Project WILD concepts to preschool and Head Start teachers, introduced habitat enhancement projects to urban school children, established a bat colony for public display, and developed a waterfowl observation and education station on Lake Erie.

The Division of Wildlife makes sure that money received through the Ohio income tax checkoff goes a long way. But additional funds are needed, for there are 116 endangered species in the state, and the public is increasingly interested in viewing and enjoying wildlife.

In most years, the Division of Wildlife receives checkoff contributions from only two to three percent of Ohioans who file income tax returns. If you are one of those contributors, *Thank You!* If this is your introduction to the check-off or you've hesitated to participate because of uncertainty about how the funds are used, we hope you are now convinced to *Do Something Wild!* Check-off for wildlife!

THE NATIONAL WATCHABLE WILDLIFE PROGRAM

The *Ohio Wildlife Viewing Guide* is part of the Watchable Wildlife Series, a national response to the growing public interest in wildlife viewing. The series is the cornerstone of the National Watchable Wildlife Program, a partnership of agencies, conservation groups, and others. This joint effort is designed to meet the growing demand for information about wildlife viewing and to develop new public support for wildlife conservation.

The Watchable Wildlife Series, coordinated nationally by Defenders of Wildlife, is much more than guidebooks. It is a program based on a simple premise: To encounter wildlife in a natural setting—a sunset flight of sandhill cranes, a white-tailed buck in velvet—is to feel awe, excitement, and wonder. These feelings inspire appreciation and understanding of the natural system and the diversity of wildlife that surround us. As these feelings grow, we are moved to take action to preserve our natural heritage.

To provide the public with opportunities to experience wildlife firsthand, Watchable Wildlife partners are working state by state to develop a nationwide network of wildlife viewing areas and to publish companion guidebooks marketed nationally as the Watchable Wildlife Series. Sites chosen for inclusion in the network are described in the guides and identified on highways and local roads with directional signs bearing a brown and white binoculars logo.

TIPS FOR VIEWING WILDLIFE

Much of the excitement of wildlife viewing comes from never knowing what you will see. Although many species are difficult to view under the best circumstances, there are several things you can do to greatly increase your chances of seeing wild animals in their natural environment.

The cardinal rule of wildlife viewing is patience. You must spend enough time in the field. If you arrive at a viewing site expecting to see every species noted in this guide, you will surely be disappointed. Review the tips below, and enjoy your time outdoors, regardless of what you see.

Prepare for your outing. Some of the sites in this guide are remote and have no facilities; review each site description before you visit, checking for warnings about services and road conditions. ALWAYS CARRY WATER, EVEN IN WINTER. Dress appropriately for the area and season. Detailed maps of many areas featured in this guide may be obtained from the Ohio Division of Wildlife. Always travel with a current road map.

Visit when animals are active. The first and last hours of daylight are usually most productive, depending on weather and season. During summer, many species hide from the midday heat. During winter, the opposite may be true—some species become more active as the day warms.

Wildlife viewing is often seasonal. Some wildlife species are present only during certain times of year. Waterfowl and shorebirds, for example, are best viewed when they migrate through Ohio in large numbers. This guide contains a wealth of information about optimal seasons for viewing selected species. Consult a field guide for additional information, or call the site owner for an update before you visit.

Use field guides. Pocket field guides are essential for positive identification of the animals named at each viewing site. Guides are available for virtually every plant and animal found in Ohio, and they contain valuable information about where animals live, what they eat, and when they rear their young.

Use binoculars or a spotting scope. Viewing aids will bridge the distance between you and wildlife. Binoculars come in different sizes, such as 7x35, 8x40, and 10x50. The first number refers to how much the animal will be magnified compared to the naked eye. A "7x" figure, for example, means that the animal will appear 7 times larger. The second number refers to the diameter of the objective lens. The larger the number, the greater amount of light will enter the lens. Larger objective lenses are better for viewing in dim light.

Move slowly and quietly. You can use several strategies for getting close to wildlife. Stay in your vehicle and wait for animals to pass by. Find a comfortable place, sit down, and remain still. Or quietly stalk wildlife. Take a few steps, then stop, look, and listen. Use your ears to locate birds or the movements of other animals. Walk into the wind if possible, and avoid brittle sticks or leaves. Use trees and vegetation as blinds. Wear dark clothes or camouflage, and consider using camouflage netting or a blind.

Enjoy wildlife at a distance. You can actually harm wildlife by getting too close. Move away from an animal if it stops feeding and raises its head sharply, appears nervous, stands up suddenly, or changes its direction of travel. Causing animals to run or move in winter forces them to use up critical energy reserves needed to survive. Leave your pets at home—they might chase or kill wildlife.

Never touch orphaned or sick animals. Young wild animals that appear to be alone usually have parents nearby. If you think an animal is wounded, sick, or abandoned, contact the site owner or the nearest wildlife agency.

Honor the rights of private landowners. Some of the viewing sites in this guide are adjacent to private land. Always ask permission before entering private property.

Honor the rights of other wildlife viewers. Keep your voice low. If others are viewing, be patient and allow them a quality experience. Leave wildlife habitat in better condition than you found it. Pick up litter and dispose of it properly.

HOW TO USE THIS GUIDE

Ohio is divided into **five wildlife districts** (central, northwest, northeast, southeast, and southwest). Each wildlife district forms a separate section of this book. Each section begins with a **wildlife district map** and a list of all the wildlife viewing sites located within that district.

Wildlife viewing sites are numbered in a consecutive pattern beginning in central Ohio. The site **description** provides a brief overview of the habitats and physiographic features found at the site, along with notes on wildlife species. It is followed by a **viewing information** section, which elaborates on wildlife species, optimal viewing times and locations, and notes on access and amenities at the viewing area. Written **directions** are supplied for each site. Always supplement the directions in this guide with an up-to-date road map.

Listed at the end of each site account is information about **ownership** of the site, along with a phone number for obtaining additional information. The **size** of the site is listed in acres. The name of the **closest town** is also included. **Facilities icons** at the bottom of the page provide important information about fees, lodging, camping, and other recreational opportunities at the site.

SITE OWNER/MANAGER ABBREVIATIONS

DOW	Division of Wildlife
DNAP	Division of Natural Areas and Preserves
DPR	Division of Parks and Recreation
DOF	Division of Forestry
USFWS	U.S. Fish and Wildlife Service
NPS	National Park Service
USFS	U.S. Forest Service

FACILITIES AND RECREATION ICONS

 Parking
 Entry Fee
 Restrooms
 Horse Trail
 Universal Access
 Hiking

 Boat Ramp
 Small Boats
 Large Boats
 Cross-Country Skiing
 Bicycling
 Camping

 Picnic
 Lodging
 Restaurant
 Nature Center
 Viewing Blind or Tower

11

ECO REGIONS OF OHIO

Hill Country

Southeastern Ohio's rugged and scenic Hill Country is home to more species of plants and animals than any other region of the state. During the past 100 years, more than 70 percent of the original forest has returned, making it the most heavily wooded part of Ohio. Woodland creatures abound in the hills, valleys, cliffs, streams, gorges, waterfalls, rock shelters, and natural bridges. Wildlife includes gray squirrels, wild turkeys, copperhead snakes, hellbender salamanders, flathead catfish, and katydids.

The Hocking Hills region of Ohio is considered by many to be the most beautiful area of the state, where autumn colors can be spectacular. Steep, heavily wooded hillsides of oak-hickory forest hide waterfalls, caves, and massive rock outcroppings such as these at Conkles Hollow State Nature Preserve located within Hocking State Forest.
ART WEBER

Gray Squirrel

Wild Turkey

Katydid

Copperhead
Snake

Flathead Catfish

Hellbender

John A. Ruthven

13

Eco Regions of Ohio

Glaciated Plateau

This picturesque region of rolling hills stretches nearly 300 miles and encompasses more people and industry than any other region of Ohio. Despite its dense human population, the Glaciated Plateau boasts great diversity of plant and animal species. Due to the repeated advance and retreat of ancient glaciers, both northern and southern species occupy the area. Wildlife includes white-tailed deer, cardinals, box turtles, dusky salamanders, brook lampreys, and monarch butterflies.

Beech-maple woodlands mix with farm fields, pastureland, and cities in Ohio's Glaciated Plateau. Besides providing wildlife habitat, these forests furnish man with maple syrup in the spring, beautiful foliage in the fall, and timber year-round.
RON AUSTING

White-tailed Deer

Cardinal

Box Turtle

Dusky Salamander

Monarch Butterfly

Least Brook Lamprey

John A Ruthven ©

15

Eco Regions of Ohio

Till Plains

Ohio's fertile western farmlands, the Till Plains, are almost exclusively agricultural and urban. Compared to other regions of the state, wildlife habitat is less diverse. Animals living here are mainly those that prefer grasslands and open spaces. Wildlife includes cottontail rabbits, Eastern meadowlarks, Eastern Plains garter snakes, gray treefrogs, smallmouth bass, and giant swallowtail butterflies.

Agriculture is one of Ohio's most important industries, providing much farmland wildlife habitat, especially in the western half of the state. At the turn of the century, nearly all of Ohio was farmland. Today about 30 percent of the original forest that once covered the state has returned.

RON AUSTING

Giant Swallowtail Butterfly

Eastern Meadowlark

Gray Treefrog

Smallmouth Bass

Cottontail Rabbit

Eastern Plains Garter Snake

17

Eco Regions of Ohio

Lake Erie and the Islands

One of Ohio's most valuable resources, this region is known not only for its world-class sportfishing, recreation, and tourism, but also for its water supply and as an industrial location. More than 3,500 square miles of Lake Erie are owned by the state of Ohio. The 12 islands in the lake are noted for their caves, sinkholes, vineyards, and orchards. More than 15,000 plant and wildlife species live within the region, including little brown bats, ring-billed gulls, Lake Erie water snakes, mudpuppy salamanders, walleyes, and Hexagenia mayflies.

Headlands Dunes State Nature Preserve, located along the south shore of Lake Erie in Lake County, is one of the last remaining sand dune-beach communities in Ohio. Atlantic coastal plant species such as sea rocket, beach pea, seaside spurge, beach grass, and purple sand grass grow on the dunes, attracting a variety of wildlife.
ART WEBER

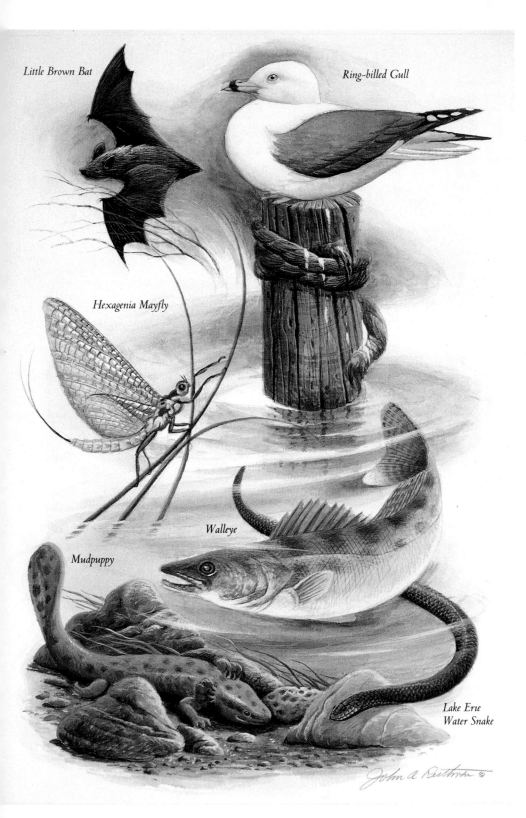

Little Brown Bat

Ring-billed Gull

Hexagenia Mayfly

Walleye

Mudpuppy

Lake Erie
Water Snake

John a Ruthven ©

ECO REGIONS OF OHIO

Lake Plain

This extremely flat region of northern Ohio is quite possibly the most important wildlife habitat in the state because of its extensive wetlands. These areas are crucial to migrating and breeding waterfowl and songbirds. In addition to thousands of acres of Lake Erie and Sandusky Bay marshes found here, the Lake Plain region includes remnants of two unique areas: the Great Black Swamp and Oak Openings. Wildlife includes muskrats, bald eagles, Blanding's turtles, leopard frogs, Western banded killifish, and green darner dragonflies.

Wetlands, such as this marsh along the western Lake Erie shoreline at Ottawa National Wildlife Refuge, are critical habitat for wildlife, especially migrating waterfowl. Ohio has lost 90 percent of its original wetlands, second only to California in percentage of wetland loss.
ART WEBER

Bald Eagle

Green Darner Dragonfly

Leopard Frog

Muskrat

Blanding's Turtle

Western Banded Killifish

21

ECO REGIONS OF OHIO

The Bluegrass

This small, triangular region in extreme southern Ohio touches only three counties: Adams, Brown, and Highland. An extension of the Bluegrass Region of Kentucky, this area is known for its prairies, caves, cedar barrens, sinkholes, and unusual plants and wildlife. More species of Ohio's endangered plants exist here than in any of the other five ecological regions. Wildlife includes Allegheny woodrats, chuck-will's-widows, fence lizards, cave salamanders, paddlefish, and olive hairstreak butterflies.

A relatively small yet very unique area of Ohio, the Bluegrass region consists of shale outcroppings, shortgrass prairies, cedar barrens, caves, and unusual plants and animals. Blooming during the summer is spike blazing star at Chaparral Prairie State Nature Preserve.

GUY DENNY/DNAP

Chuck-will's-widow

Cave
Salamander

Fence Lizard

Allegheny Woodrat

Olive Hairstreak
Butterfly

Paddlefish

John A. Ruthven ©

White-tailed deer are found statewide and are one of the most frequently seen and easily identified wildlife species in Ohio. Bucks drop their antlers late each winter and grow a new set by late summer. Antler size and growth is a combination of three factors: age, nutrition, and genetics.

JIM ROETZEL

OHIO
WILDLIFE VIEWING AREAS

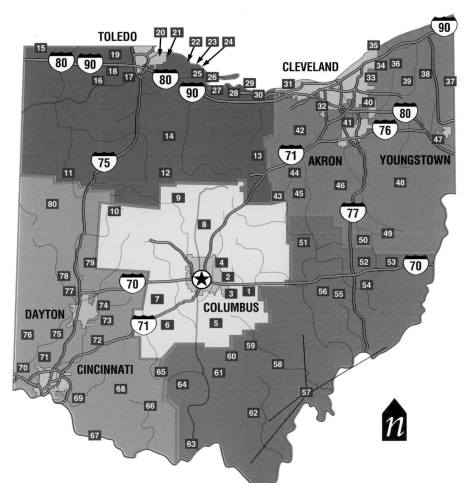

Ohio is divided into five Wildlife Viewing Districts. Each district is a separate section in this guide. Viewing sites are numbered consecutively and follow a general pattern in each district.

00 Wildlife Viewing Site
- District One: Central Ohio
- District Two: Northwest Ohio
- District Three: Northeast Ohio
- District Four: Southeast Ohio
- District Five: Southwest Ohio

WILDLIFE VIEWING AREA

As you travel in Ohio and other states, look for these special highway signs identifying wildlife viewing sites. These signs will help guide you to viewing areas. Note: be sure to read the written directions provided with each site in this book—highway signs may refer to more than one site along a particular route.

DISTRICT ONE: CENTRAL OHIO

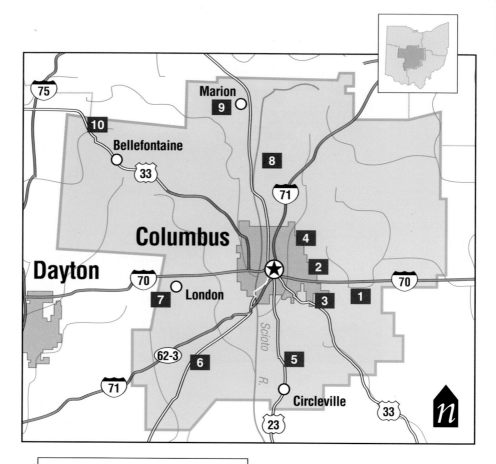

WILDLIFE VIEWING SITES
1. Hebron Fish Hatchery
2. Blacklick Woods Metro Park
3. Pickerington Ponds Wetland Wildlife Refuge
4. Walden Waterfowl Refuge
5. Stage's Pond State Nature Preserve
6. Deer Creek Wildlife Area
7. London Fish Hatchery
8. Delaware Wildlife Area
9. Big Island Wildlife Area
10. Indian Lake State Park

1. HEBRON FISH HATCHERY

Description: Hebron Hatchery raises walleye, saugeye, bluegill, channel catfish, hybrid striped bass, largemouth bass, and fathead minnows. The facility is open to the public year-round, Monday through Friday, 8 a.m. to 4:30 p.m.; you'll see the most fish in spring. Hebron is a birding hot spot—more than 252 species have been recorded at numerous ponds and wetlands.

Viewing Information: Approximately 2.5 miles of nature trails wind through wildlife habitats. Three wetlands and 63 fish-rearing ponds attract waterfowl, shorebirds, and furbearers. In spring and fall, the "Big Woods" and "Old Field" areas are excellent places to see wood warblers. The hatchery is adjacent to Buckeye Lake and the historic Ohio & Erie Canal, where you can see more aquatic wildlife.

Directions: *From Hebron, follow Canal Road 2 miles south to the hatchery entrance.*

Ownership: DOW, call 1-800-WILDLIFE for a free brochure

Size: 217 acres   **Closest Town:** Hebron

Largemouth bass, common statewide and a favorite in Ohio farm ponds, are only one of several species of fish raised at the Hebron Fish Hatchery near Buckeye Lake east of Columbus. Also reared at Hebron for stocking into Ohio Lakes and streams are walleye, saugeye, bluegill, channel catfish, and hybrid striped bass. In addition, fathead minnows are raised to be fed to predatory muskellunge growing at London and Kincaid state hatcheries. The 63 rearing ponds and wetlands at Hebron are a magnet for wildlife, especially migratory birds. More than 252 species of birds have been recorded here. RON KEIL

2. BLACKLICK WOODS METRO PARK

Description: A swamp-forest wildlife community is the unique feature of this park near Columbus. The portion called Walter A. Tucker State Nature Preserve is also a registered National Natural Landmark. Beech-maple and elm-ash-maple woods are home to abundant wildflowers and wildlife. The area's 2.5 miles of foot trails include a paved 0.7-mile loop for people with mobility disabilities. Wheelchair accessible restrooms are provided.

Viewing Information: The nature center's wide viewing windows, with songbird and waterfowl feeders nearby, overlook a pond and swamp. Watch for white-tailed deer, raccoons, foxes, gray squirrels, and mink. From spring through early fall, you can see herons, wood ducks, and snapping turtles. Woodpeckers, tufted titmice, blue jays, and song sparrows are common year-round. Canada geese and mallards are regular visitors, but more abundant fall through spring. Look for waterfowl at Ashton Pond near the park entrance. A wooden viewing deck with seating is available .

Directions: From Columbus, take Interstate 70 east to State Route 256. Turn north on State Route 256 and go 1 mile to Livingston Avenue. Turn west on Livingston Avenue and go 0.75 mile to the park entrance located on the south side of the road, past the golf course.

Ownership: Metropolitan Park District of Columbus and Franklin County (614) 891-0700

Size: 632 acres
Closest Town: Reynoldsburg

3. PICKERINGTON PONDS WETLAND WILDLIFE REFUGE

Description: A wide, shallow glacial kettle pond surrounded by upland grasslands attracts migrating Canada geese, black ducks, mallards, and many other species of waterfowl and shorebirds during spring and fall. In summer, you can see songbirds; painted, snapping, softshell, and box turtles; water snakes; and frogs. A heronry of approximately 40 nests offers good viewing.

Viewing Information: Parking and a barrier-free observation shelter are located at the Bowen Road observation area along the west side of the pond. Additional viewing and parking are available along Wright Road to the north. While slowly driving the roads around the perimeter, be alert for ring-necked pheasants, Eastern meadowlarks, cottontail rabbits, white-tailed deer, and other species of upland wildlife. Birds of prey frequent the vicinity. Telephone (614) 895-6222 to hear a recorded message of weekly waterfowl sightings at Pickerington Ponds and Thoreau Lake at nearby Blendon Woods Metropark.

Directions: From Columbus, take U.S. Route 33 east toward Lancaster approximately 6 miles to Bowen Road. Turn north. The Bowen Road observation area is on the right at 2.4 miles.

Ownership: Metropolitan Park District of Columbus and Franklin County (614) 891-0700

Size: 456 acres   **Closest Town:** Canal Winchester

4. WALDEN WATERFOWL REFUGE

Description: This viewing site, featuring 11-acre Thoreau Lake, is the main attraction of Blendon Woods Metro Park just east of Columbus. The lake is managed exclusively to attract waterfowl for public viewing. You can see ducks, geese, and other water birds from the cover of two elevated, carpeted observation shelters. Spotting scopes are available when a park naturalist is at the blinds. Waterfowl viewing is best autumn through spring. Several hundred to several thousand ducks and geese pass through during peak migrations. An aeration system keeps the lake open during winter, and birds are fed corn to keep them in the area.

Viewing Information: You can see Canada geese and mallards every day. During migration, as many as 16 waterfowl species pass through. Telephone (614) 895-6222 to hear a recorded message of weekly waterfowl sightings at Thoreau Lake and also nearby Pickerington Ponds. Two miles of nature trails wind across ridges and through ravines of beech-maple forest. Abundant wildflowers brighten these trails during spring. Year-round residents include cardinals, red fox, great horned owls, salamanders, and squirrels—red, gray, and fox. Stop by the nature center while you're here.

Directions: From Columbus, follow State Route 161 east 1.5 miles from Interstate 270. The park entrance is on the south side of the road.

Ownership: Metropolitan Park District of Columbus and Franklin County (614) 891-0700

Size: 118 acres
Closest Town: Westerville or Columbus

Mallards are present at Walden Waterfowl Refuge year-round, as they are at most water areas throughout the state. The second most common breeding duck in Ohio behind the wood duck, mallards prefer to make their nests on the ground in dense, grassy cover within 100 feet of water. Hens are a mottled brown color, while drakes sport an easily identifiable dark green head. PAUL B. SWARMER

5. STAGE'S POND STATE NATURE PRESERVE

Description: If you are looking for an out-of-the-way, less crowded wildlife viewing area in south-central Ohio, this is a good choice. A 30-acre kettle lake, remnant of Ice Age glaciers that covered most of Ohio, distinguishes this site. As the glacier receded, an immense chunk of ice broke off and remained behind. When this land-locked ice mass finally melted, it left a large, water-filled depression—Stage's Pond. There are two low, marshy areas nearby as well as field and woodland habitats.

Viewing Information: A covered wildlife viewing blind overlooks the two marshes. You can see wood ducks, great blue herons, red-winged blackbirds, and other water birds. A hike to the pond takes you through field habitat for upland game birds such as ring-necked pheasants, bobwhite quail, and woodcock. At the pond, look for turtles, dragonflies, kingfishers, and swallows during summer, and ducks and geese during fall and spring migration. Ospreys are occasional. A heronry is nearby. The adjacent oak-hickory woodlands are home to songbirds and several species of raptors such as Cooper's hawks and great horned owls.

Directions: *From Circleville, follow U.S. Route 23 approximately 5 miles north to Haggerty Road, then 1.5 miles east to the entrance.*

Ownership: DNAP (614) 265-6463

Size: 178 acres   **Closest Town:** Circleville

Although it is possible to see a green heron anywhere near water in Ohio, these wading birds are most numerous in northeastern counties and also in western Lake Erie marshes. At the turn of the century they were considered common summer residents, but wetland drainage and stream channelization have significantly reduced their numbers within the state, particularly in western Ohio. L. WEST

6. DEER CREEK WILDLIFE AREA

Description: This area, adjacent to Deer Creek State Park and 1,277-acre Deer Creek Lake in south-central Ohio, is known for open grasslands and associated upland wildlife. Large fields of switchgrass and timothy support healthy populations of ring-necked pheasants, grassland-nesting songbirds, and raptors. A 75-acre marsh at the southern end of the wildlife area, along Dick Road, provides habitat for waterfowl, shorebirds, and furbearers. The wooded uplands along Deer Creek are home to white-tailed deer, raccoons, and squirrels, both fox and red.

Viewing Information: Game birds and other grassland wildlife thrive here. Birds of prey include red-tailed hawks, Northern harriers, and American kestrels. Large numbers of turkey vultures roost on the area. Rare and unusual birds include ospreys, cormorants, and great egrets in summer, and short-eared owls and sandhill cranes in winter. Late winter and spring are the best times to view waterfowl at the marsh and Deer Creek Lake. Watch for beaver along Deer Creek and its tributaries. Deer Creek Wildlife Area is open to hunters during regular hunting seasons.

Directions: From Mount Sterling, follow State Route 207 approximately 3 miles south.

Ownership: DOW, call 1-800-WILDLIFE for a free area map

Size: 3,710 acres   **Closest Town:** Mount Sterling

7. LONDON FISH HATCHERY

Description: Rainbow trout, golden rainbow trout, brown trout, and muskellunge are raised here; more than half a million fingerlings are produced annually. London boasts its own strain of rainbow trout and is known at home and abroad for its technique of raising young walleyes on artificial diets. Fish are just part of the hatchery's viewing opportunity; wild creatures are attracted to the 34 outdoor rearing ponds.

Viewing Information: Great blue herons, muskrats, mink, water snakes, turtles, frogs, toads, crayfish, and dragonflies are among the wetland wildlife species living at London Fish Hatchery. Small groves of pine and hardwoods attract woodland songbirds. The hatchery is open to the public from 8 a.m. to 5 p.m., Monday through Friday. Don't miss the fish in the three outdoor display tanks.

Directions: From State Route 40 northwest of London, follow Roberts Mill Road S.W. approximately 2.5 miles south.

Ownership: DOW, call 1-800-WILDLIFE for a free brochure

Size: 82 acres   **Closest Town:** London

8. DELAWARE WILDLIFE AREA

Description: This large area in central Ohio is adjacent to Delaware State Park and 1,330-acre Delaware Lake. It is distinguished by farmland, grassland, brushland, and woodland wildlife habitats. Approximately 50 ponds and a 159-acre marsh provide excellent birding. The Ohio Division of Wildlife's upland wildlife research headquarters, called the Olentangy Wildlife Research Station, is located here.

Viewing Information: Ring-necked pheasants, cottontail rabbits, fox squirrels, groundhogs, raccoons, muskrats, mink, skunks, foxes, and opossums are common. You can see ducks, geese, and shorebirds at the lake, marsh, or ponds, especially during spring migration. Red-tailed hawks, American kestrels, and Northern harriers frequent open fields and woodlots. Turkey vultures soar during warmer months. A heronry is located in the area. Rare or unusual birds include bald eagles, Northern goshawks, ospreys, king rails, snowy owls, long-eared owls, great egrets, cattle egrets, and sandhill cranes. Delaware Wildlife Area is open to hunters during regular hunting seasons.

Directions: *From Delaware, follow U.S. Route 23 approximately 10 miles north to State Route 229. Turn east on State Route 229 and follow it just over 3 miles to Horseshoe Road, then south approximately 0.25 mile to the area headquarters.*

Ownership: DOW, call 1-800-WILDLIFE for a free area map

Size: 4,670 acres   **Closest Town:** Waldo

Monarch butterflies are known for their travels, migrating up to 2,000 miles from Canada to Mexico in the fall. In spring, females returning north travel in relays, laying their eggs along the way as new generations replace the old. The cycle from egg to butterfly takes about a month.
GARY MESLAROS

9. BIG ISLAND WILDLIFE AREA

Description: This was one of the largest wetland prairies in the state at the time of settlement. The distinguishing feature is a 382-acre man-made marsh occupied by waterfowl, shorebirds, wading birds, songbirds, turtles, frogs, and insects. Some birders think this wetland complex is the finest in central Ohio for avian diversity. The rest of the area is grain cropfields and meadows interspersed with brushy fencerows and woodlots. Several fields have been planted to prairie grasses, and future plans include planting more than 1,000 acres of grasses and forbs. The headwaters of the Scioto River snake along the south edge of the area.

Viewing Information: Several parking lots along Marion County Road 37 offer good overviews of the marsh. If you care to hike, follow the elevated dikes to see Canada geese, mallards, wood ducks, and other waterfowl, especially spring and fall. In the woodlots you can see fox squirrels, chipmunks, and songbirds. Open fields provide habitat for ring-necked pheasants, cottontail rabbits, grasshopper sparrows, savannah sparrows, horned larks, and Northern harriers. Endangered species have been seen at the marsh: American bitterns, least bitterns, and king rails. Bald eagles from nearby Killdeer Plains Wildlife Area occasionally make an appearance. Big Island Wildlife Area is open to hunters during regular hunting seasons.

Directions: From Marion, follow State Route 95 approximately 5 miles west.

Ownership: DOW, call 1-800-WILDLIFE for a free area map

Size: 5,000 acres   **Closest Town:** New Bloomington

Backyards are great places to watch wildlife. A backyard that provides food, water, and shelter for wildlife may be certified as an official "Backyard for Wildlife Site." To apply for certification, contact the Ohio Division of Wildlife.

10. INDIAN LAKE STATE PARK

Description: This large lake in west-central Ohio is a magnet for migrating birds, especially water birds. Twenty-nine miles of irregular shoreline and 69 islands make Indian Lake ideal wetland wildlife habitat. Thousands of ducks and geese of many species move through the area during migrations, with some (especially mallards, Canada geese, and wood ducks) remaining in the spring to nest. Other water birds such as herons, egrets, gulls, sandpipers, and shorebirds are common.

Viewing Information: Some of the best wildlife viewing opportunities from shore are at Pew Island and the Moundwood area on the east side of the lake; west of Russells Point along the south shore; and the Old Field Island area along the west bank. On the north side of the lake, visitors enjoy seeing wildlife up close along two self-guided canoe trails. One trail starts near the park campground and continues around Blackhawk Island for about 3 miles. The other canoe trail is in the Pony Island area and is approximately 5 miles long. Portions of Indian Lake are open to hunters during regular hunting seasons.

Directions: Located along U.S. Route 33, 10 miles northwest of Bellefontaine.

Ownership: DPR (937) 843-2717

Size: 6,452 acres   **Closest Town:** Lakeview or Russells Point

Do Something Wild! *The Ohio Division of Wildlife's state income tax checkoff program receives about half a million dollars annually in donations from Ohio taxpayers. This money allows the Division to work with and benefit specific endangered species and nongame wildlife.*

DISTRICT TWO: NORTHWEST OHIO

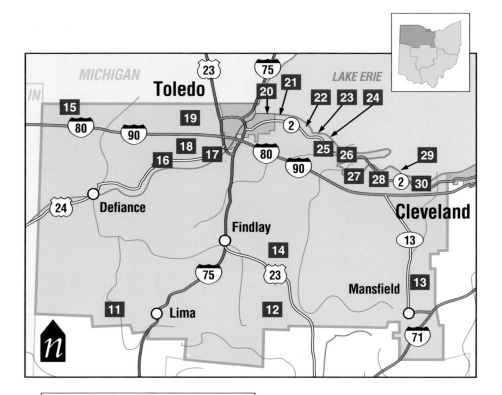

WILDLIFE VIEWING SITES
11. Kendrick Woods
12. Killdeer Plains Wildlife Area
13. Fowler Woods State Nature Preserve
14. Springville Marsh State Nature Preserve
15. Lake La Su An Wildlife Area
16. Maumee State Forest
17. Farnsworth Metropark
18. Oak Openings Preserve Metropark
19. Irwin Prairie State Nature Preserve
20. Maumee Bay State Park
21. Mallard Club Marsh Wildlife Area
22. Metzger Marsh Wildlife Area
23. Ottawa National Wildlife Refuge
24. Magee Marsh Wildlife Area
25. Toussaint Wildlife Area
26. Little Portage Wildlife Area
27. Pickerel Creek Wildlife Area
28. Resthaven Wildlife Area
29. Sheldon Marsh State Nature Preserve
30. Old Woman Creek National Estuarine
    Research Reserve and State Nature Preserve

11. KENDRICK WOODS

Description: Allen County's largest remaining woodland contains a designated state nature preserve. Swamp-forest creatures such as spotted salamanders are common. You can see animals of the grasslands near the restored 5-acre tallgrass prairie. View wetland species from an observation blind overlooking a 6-acre wetland beside the Auglaize River.

Viewing Information: Stroll along the 0.33-mile, handicap-accessible "All People Trail" boardwalk, or hike 5 miles of trails. Unusual plants include swamp saxifrage, goldenseal, Virginia bluebell, blue cohosh, green dragon, and fire pink. You'll find an artesian sulphur spring along the South Trail, next to Six Mile Creek. Watch for wildlife in and around the 1.25-acre pond near the parking area.

Directions: *Located 0.5 mile north of State Route 81 on Defiance Trail, 4 miles northeast of Spencerville.*

Ownership: Johnny Appleseed Metropolitan Park District (419) 221-1232

Size: 219 acres   **Closest Town:** Spencerville

Red-winged blackbirds are always one of the first birds to arrive in Ohio each spring. Look for males staking out and defending mating territories as early as late February and early March. Females are a mottled brown color and build their nests in dense grasses. During the 19th century, red-wings in Ohio were found almost exclusively near cattail marshes. However, as wetlands were drained, breeding pairs began using upland habitats such as hayfields and pastures. Today, red-winged blackbirds use upland meadows as frequently as wetlands.

JIM ROETZEL

12. KILLDEER PLAINS WILDLIFE AREA

Description: This large, diverse wildlife area in north-central Ohio is a mixture of grassland, brushland, woodland, marsh, swamp, and pond wildlife habitats. The area features a bald eagle nest and a heronry, and has been the traditional winter hunting grounds of short-eared and long-eared owls for decades. Situated in a natural basin of flat, poorly drained prairie soils, Killdeer boasts 1,100 acres of marsh, a 285-acre upground reservoir, and 125 ponds that vary in size from 50 acres to less than one acre. In fall, during peak migration, observers have counted 30,000 ducks and 11,000 Canada geese.

Viewing Information: Killdeer is an excellent birding spot. Of particular interest are the spring migrations of shorebirds and warblers and the fall migrations of waterfowl and hawks. Large numbers of black-bellied plovers and golden plovers pause en route to their Arctic nesting grounds. The fall passage of red-tailed and other hawks can be spectacular. Monarch butterflies migrate through in mid-September. In fields and along ditch banks, you'll notice tallgrass prairie remnants, habitat for the massasauga or swamp rattlesnake and endangered Eastern Plains garter snake. A portion of the area is a designated wildlife refuge and is closed to visitors, but much wildlife is visible from the roads, especially white-tailed deer. Killdeer Plains Wildlife Area is open to hunters during regular hunting seasons.

Directions: *From Harpster, follow State Route 294 approximately 2 miles west.*

Ownership: DOW, call 1-800-WILDLIFE for a free area map

Size: 8,627 acres **Closest Town:** Upper Sandusky

As their name implies, Eastern meadowlarks prefer grasslands. Their distinctive yellow and black breast patterns make them easy to identify along rural roadways. More numerous in the reclaimed strip mine areas of eastern Ohio, meadowlarks spend much of their spring days singing from fence posts or other perches.
TIM DANIEL

13. FOWLER WOODS STATE NATURE PRESERVE

Description: This north-central Ohio site boasts a climax forest of beech, maple, oak, tulip, and ash trees, many of them 100 to 200 years old. They contain an estimated 1 million board feet of lumber! Wildflowers are spectacular during April and May. Boardwalk trails guide you through most of the area. Woodland songbirds and birds of prey are common. Eight species of snakes (none venomous), eight species of frogs and toads, and four species of woodland salamanders have been identified.

Viewing Information: Mammals include red and fox squirrels, chipmunks, cottontail rabbits, groundhogs, raccoons, opossums, red and gray foxes, and white-tailed deer. A viewing tower overlooks a buttonbush swamp and surrounding swamp-forest. The area comes alive with the sounds of spring peepers and chorus frogs during mating season. Warblers, flycatchers, and woodpeckers make their home here. Birds of prey include red-tailed, sharp-shinned, and Cooper's hawks, as well as barred owls. Turkey vultures soar on warm summer days.

Directions: *From Olivesburg, follow Olivesburg-Fitchville Road 6 miles north to the entrance.*

Ownership: DNAP (419) 981-6319

Size: 133 acres   **Closest Town:** Olivesburg or Mansfield

14. SPRINGVILLE MARSH STATE NATURE PRESERVE

Description: This area is a remnant of the once vast Big Spring Prairie. It is one of the largest inland wetlands in the Till Plains of northwestern Ohio. Several Canadian and Atlantic Coastal Plain plant species became established here shortly after the last Ice Age. Fen orchids, bottle gentian, Kalm's lobelia, and little yellow sedge grow along the boardwalk. The pond attracts muskrats, mink, raccoons, frogs, waterfowl, and wading birds. Spotted turtles, rare to this preserve, are seen occasionally.

Viewing Information: A 2,600-foot boardwalk through corridors of cattails leads you to a wildlife viewing blind for a close look at the marsh's inhabitants; a viewing tower 10 feet high provides a panoramic outlook. The trail leads back to the parking lot through a wet woods of huge cottonwoods, hackberry, and wild cherry trees harboring warblers, goldfinches, cardinals, wrens, sparrows, and birds of prey. Usually, a spring visit is best because of the abundance of water then.

Directions: *From Carey, travel 3.5 miles north on U.S. Route 23 and State Route 199 to Township Road 24. Turn west and go 1 mile to the area entrance.*

Ownership: DNAP (419) 981-6319

Size: 201 acres   **Closest Town:** Carey

15. LAKE LA SU AN WILDLIFE AREA

Description: This area, in the gently rolling hills of extreme northwestern Ohio, is composed of small lakes and ponds surrounded by upland fields and woodlands. The west branch of the St. Joseph River flows through the center.

Viewing Information: Healthy populations of largemouth bass and bluegills thrive in most of the 14 lakes and ponds. Largemouth bass densities are the highest in the Midwest. (Fishing is by special permit and reservation only.) Ring-necked pheasants flourish in the old fields. Sandhill cranes rest and feed during spring and fall migration, as do marsh hawks and short-eared owls. An unusual resident is the Northern copper-belly snake. Lake La Su An Wildlife Area is open to hunters during regular hunting seasons.

Directions: *Follow County Road 7 approximately 3 miles north from U.S. Route 20 in northwest Williams County, then 0.25 mile west on County Road R.*

Ownership: DOW, call 1-800-WILDLIFE for a free area map

Size: 2,100 acres   **Closest Town:** Pioneer

16. MAUMEE STATE FOREST

Description: This state forest in the unique Oak Openings region of north-western Ohio is home to rare and diverse plant and animal communities. Sections of the forest spread over several miles and three counties. The topography is extremely flat. The most unusual habitat here is a wet sedge meadow.

Viewing Information: The muck farm area (also designated as a dog training grounds), located along Henry County Road 2 south of Washington Township Road V, is a good place to see woodland and field birds, especially woodcock mating flights in the spring. Bridle trails are available. Oak Openings Preserve Metropark to the northeast is a must-see. Maumee State Forest is open to hunters during regular hunting seasons. An all-purpose vehicle (APV) area is also located within the forest.

Directions: *From Whitehouse, the Forest Headquarters is located approximately 7 miles west on Henry County Road D.*

Ownership: DOF (419) 822-3052

Size: 3,068 acres   **Closest Town:** Neapolis

17.   FARNSWORTH METROPARK

Description: This long, narrow metropark parallels the north shore of the Maumee River southwest of Toledo. Many consider it the most scenic site in the Maumee River Valley. The Roche de Bout Island rock formation is steeped in Indian legend and was used as a ceremonial site. Fort Deposit once stood on the bluffs above the river. Here, General "Mad" Anthony Wayne drilled his troops in preparation for the 1794 Battle of Fallen Timbers, one of the most important battles of the fledgling United States.

Viewing Information: Roche de Bout Rapids, immediately below Missionary Island, is the wildlife viewing highlight of this park. The 0.5-mile stretch of whitewater is an excellent birding area, especially in late summer and fall, when more of the rocks are exposed for perching sites. Whether you sit on the bank and enjoy a picnic lunch or launch a canoe and paddle the river, you are likely to see gulls, great blue herons, great egrets, killdeer, belted kingfishers, and a variety of other shorebirds, water birds, and wading birds. Look for a rock fracture zone known as Bowling Green Fault in an overhanging cliff just north of the park along the river's shore.

Directions: *From Toledo, follow Interstate 475 to U.S. Route 24 on the southwest edge of the city. Take U.S. Route 24 approximately 6 miles south to the Roche de Bout area of Farnsworth Metropark, just south of Waterville.*

Ownership: Metropolitan Park District of the Toledo Area (419) 878-7641 or (419) 535-3050

Size: 100 acres   **Closest Town:** Waterville

Ohio currently has 116 species of wildlife on its endangered species list, including mammals, birds, reptiles, amphibians, fishes, mollusks, butterflies, moths, and beetles. Many of these species inhabit the wildlife viewing sites listed in this guide.

18. OAK OPENINGS PRESERVE METROPARK

Description: The unique Oak Openings region of northwestern Ohio is composed of oak savannahs and sand dunes created by an ancient glacial lake. Approximately 25 miles long and 5 miles wide, the area boasts more rare plants and animals than any other place in the state. Oak Openings Preserve is well known to Ohio's serious birders. Spring vulture-watch programs are open to the public.

Viewing Information: Mallard Lake, along Oak Openings Parkway, is a good place to begin your visit because all the hiking trails start here. Songbirds dwell in the surrounding white and black oak forest. Unusual are the lark sparrow, blue grosbeak, and prairie, golden, and blue-winged warblers. The sand dunes along Girdham Road are worth a stop. The park is one of the few places in Ohio where you might see a badger! The area is home to unusual salamanders: tiger, blue-spotted, Tremblay's, and red-backed. If you want to escape crowds, portions of Maumee State Forest are located immediately southwest of Oak Openings Preserve Metropark.

Directions: *From Toledo, follow State Route 2 approximately 8 miles west to State Route 295. Turn south on State Route 295 and follow it just over 2 miles to Oak Openings Parkway.*

Ownership: Metropolitan Park District of the Toledo Area (419) 535-3050 or (419) 826-6463

Size: 3,668 acres   **Closest Town:** Swanton or Whitehouse

Extirpated from the state in 1988, the Karner blue butterfly is both a state and federally endangered species. The Ohio Division of Wildlife plans to reintroduce this species to the Oak Openings region of northwest Ohio sometime in the near future.

L. WEST

19. IRWIN PRAIRIE STATE NATURE PRESERVE

Description: This is one of the finest examples of sedge-meadow habitat remaining in Ohio. Mallards and wood ducks nest and feed on this wet prairie. Some of the more unusual summer birds include pied-billed grebes, least bitterns, Virginia and sora rails, and common snipe. Songbirds include marsh wrens, yellow warblers, sedge wrens, alder flycatchers, veeries, and swamp sparrows. Muskrats, mink, raccoons, skunks, opossums, red foxes, and white-tailed deer feed at dawn and dusk. The rare spotted turtle inhabits the area.

Viewing Information: The best times to visit are spring and early summer, when water is abundant. An extensive boardwalk leads from the parking lot at Bancroft Road through a dense shrub swamp. On the east side of Irwin Road lies a large sedge meadow. The boardwalk continues through a pin oak woods to an observation deck overlooking a grass meadow which is a shallow lake most of the year. Early in the season, waterfowl and other aquatic wildlife, such as fairy shrimp, are visible from the deck. Observe woodcock courtship flights on most spring evenings.

Directions: *From Toledo, follow U.S. Route 20 west to State Route 295. Turn south on State Route 295 and follow it 1 mile to Bancroft Road. Turn east on Bancroft Road and go 3 miles to the entrance on the south side of the road.*

Ownership: DNAP (419) 445-1775

Size: 215 acres   **Closest Town:** Holland

Ohio's Blanding's turtle is limited primarily to the northern counties along Lake Erie, where it inhabits marshy shorelines, inland streams, and wet meadows. Although essentially aquatic, the Blanding's turtle often wanders about on land, but seldom far from water. Its most distinctive field mark is its bright yellow throat and chin.
GARY MESLAROS

42

20. MAUMEE BAY STATE PARK

Description: Begin your visit at Trautman Nature Center, 2,000 square feet of state-of-the-art interpretive exhibits that include interactive computer displays, a 55-seat auditorium, and wildlife feeding stations visible from viewing windows. Located in northwestern Ohio along the south shore of Lake Erie's Maumee Bay, this park is on the spring and fall migration route for hundreds of thousands of birds. Inundated swamp-forest is the primary habitat, but a large grassland ecotype, the last in this part of Ohio, exists here too. More than 300 species of birds have been recorded, including bald eagles and snowy owls. Overnight accommodations include cabins and a lodge overlooking Lake Erie.

Viewing Information: Spring and fall, take the boardwalk from the nature center to view neotropical migrants such as warblers, flycatchers, vireos, tanagers, and orioles. Multitudes of waterfowl create a spectacular display November through April. Possibly, you'll see migrating tundra swans. Hundreds of monarch butterflies are raised, tagged, and released here each year. Maumee Bay State Park, Mallard Club Marsh Wildlife Area, and Cedar Point National Wildlife Refuge form a large, contiguous wetland habitat.

Directions: From Interstate 280 just east of Toledo, follow State Route 2 for 6 miles east to North Curtice Road and turn north. The park entrance is 3 miles ahead.

Ownership: DPR, Trautman Nature Center: (419) 836-9117; Park Office: (419) 836-7305. For lodge or cabin reservations call 1-800-AT-A-PARK

Size: 1,529 acres   **Closest Town:** Toledo

21. MALLARD CLUB MARSH WILDLIFE AREA

Description: This area of the Lake Erie marsh region, formerly owned by a private duck hunting club, was purchased by the Ohio Division of Wildlife. Primarily wetland, it is bordered on the west by Maumee Bay State Park, on the north by Maumee Bay, and on the northeast by Cedar Point National Wildlife Refuge. Thus, waterfowl and other marshland species abound.

Viewing Information: Several parking lots along Cedar Point Road on the southern edge of the area give good views of the marsh. Viewers who walk the miles of dikes see waterfowl, wading birds, open-water birds, and birds of prey. Abundant during the warmer months are snakes, turtles, frogs, and insects. Mallard Club Marsh Wildlife Area is open to hunters during regular hunting seasons.

Directions: From Oregon, follow State Route 2 approximately 6 miles east to either Cousino Road or Decant Road. Follow either road north to the area.

Ownership: DOW, call 1-800-WILDLIFE for a free area map

Size: 410 acres   **Closest Town:** Oregon

22. METZGER MARSH WILDLIFE AREA

Description: This part of the Lake Erie shoreline makes a good drive-through tour. Much of the wetland is visible from the elevated causeway. You can see open-water birds from the fishing pier jutting into Lake Erie or from the outer barrier dike. Recently, the outer dike was restored, improving habitat for wetland wildlife. Fluctuating water levels due to shifting winds make this a diverse, ever-changing marsh.

Viewing Information: During spring and fall, Metzger Marsh attracts large numbers of mallards, black ducks, and widgeons; fewer numbers of teal, pintails, gadwalls, wood ducks, canvasbacks, redheads, and coots. Tundra swans inhabit the area March through May. Great blue herons, great egrets, bitterns, black-crowned night herons, green herons, cormorants, and many species of shorebirds thrive. A bald eagle's nest is nearby.

Directions: *From Toledo, follow State Route 2 approximately 13 miles east.*

Ownership: DOW, call 1-800-WILDLIFE for a free area map

Size: 560 acres   **Closest Town:** Toledo

Seen most often at Metzger Marsh during spring and fall migrations, canvasbacks are part of a grouping of waterfowl known as diving ducks. Unlike puddle ducks, which tip up when feeding or simply forage at the water's surface, diving ducks sometimes dive as deep as 70 feet under water in search of food. A prized game bird, the canvasback is most often confused in identification with the redhead duck, which has similar coloration but lacks the wedge-shaped head of the "Can." Canvasbacks nest in the prairie pothole regions of the United States and Canada.
RON AUSTING

23. OTTAWA NATIONAL WILDLIFE REFUGE

Description: This refuge, coupled with state-owned Magee Marsh Wildlife Area to the east, may be Ohio's premier birding location. More than 274 bird species are listed as regular visitors; another 49 species are seen rarely. The refuge receives dramatic flights of migratory birds such as wood warblers in spring and waterfowl in fall. Bald eagles show up throughout the year. They nest from February to July.

Viewing Information: Seven miles of interpretive trails follow the dike system around and through the refuge's primarily marshland habitat. A wildlife observation platform is located along the Blue Heron Trail near the refuge office. This birder's paradise is also home to white-tailed deer, opossums, raccoons, groundhogs, red foxes, skunks, muskrats, mink, cottontail rabbits, and fox squirrels. Reptiles, amphibians, and dragonflies abound during warmer months. Nearby Cedar Point and West Sister Island national wildlife refuges are permit-only.

Directions: *From Toledo, follow State Route 2 approximately 15 miles east to the refuge entrance on the north side of the road.*

Ownership: USFWS (419) 898-0014

Size: 4,683 acres   **Closest Town:** Oak Harbor

NORTHWEST OHIO

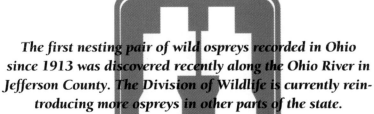

The first nesting pair of wild ospreys recorded in Ohio since 1913 was discovered recently along the Ohio River in Jefferson County. The Division of Wildlife is currently reintroducing more ospreys in other parts of the state.

24. MAGEE MARSH WILDLIFE AREA

Description: This area and adjacent Ottawa National Wildlife Refuge form the most important wetland complex in the Lake Erie marsh region and quite possibly the best birding location in Ohio. Water birds and songbirds flourish; thousands of neotropical migrants pass through in spring and fall. Birds of prey are abundant during migration. A bald eagle nest is located on the marsh and eagles are present year-round. Take an auto tour from the Sportsmen's Migratory Bird Center to the barrier beach along Lake Erie, following an elevated dike through open marshland. Magee Marsh is headquarters for Ohio Division of Wildlife waterfowl and furbearer research and management programs.

Viewing Information: An observation tower near the visitor center and museum gives a good overview of the marsh. Major waterfowl species include mallards, black ducks, widgeons, and Canada geese. You can see tundra swans during migration. Along the road to the beach, look for dragonflies, damselflies, Blanding's and painted turtles, bullfrogs, green frogs, herons, bitterns, cormorants, and shorebirds. A 0.8-mile boardwalk begins near the beach parking area and is an excellent place to view songbirds, especially during migration. See rafts of waterfowl 100,000 strong offshore during winter. Magee Marsh Wildlife Area is open to waterfowl hunting by permit only during regular hunting seasons.

Directions: *From Port Clinton, follow State Route 2 west 17 miles to Crane Creek State Park and Magee Marsh Wildlife Area. The entrance is on the east side of Route 2.*

Ownership: DOW, call 1-800-WILDLIFE for a free area map; Sportsmen's Migratory Bird Center (419) 898-0960

Size: 2,160 acres   **Closest Town:** Oak Harbor

The boardwalk bird trail at Magee Marsh is considered by many to be the best birding location in Ohio. In spring, migrating songbirds "stage" on the forested beach ridge in preparation for crossing Lake Erie. More than 156 species of songbirds, including 35 species of warblers, have been recorded at Magee. Waterfowl can also be seen by the thousands both spring and fall, and raptors are abundant.
RON KEIL

25. TOUSSAINT WILDLIFE AREA

Description: If you are in the Lake Erie marsh region, this small wildlife area along a bend of the Toussaint River is worth a quick stop. Look for puddle ducks, woodcocks, snipes, sora and Virginia rails, plovers, herons, bitterns, yellowlegs, and other wading and water birds. Mammals such as muskrats are abundant.

Viewing Information: The parking area along State Route 19 gives a good overview of the river and its open-water birds. Access to the marsh is from a parking lot along Township Road 92 at the southern edge of the area, 0.5 mile west of State Route 19. Toussaint Wildlife Area is open to hunters during regular hunting seasons.

Directions: From Oak Harbor, follow State Route 19 north approximately 5 miles.

Ownership: DOW, call 1-800-WILDLIFE for a free area map

Size: 236 acres   **Closest Town:** Oak Harbor

26. LITTLE PORTAGE WILDLIFE AREA

Description: Here is a secluded, less developed viewing site. This river marsh in the Lake Erie marsh region is bounded on the west by the Little Portage River and on the north by the Portage River. Approximately two-thirds of the area is wetlands. Eighty acres of upland habitat are maintained in a mixture of grasslands, grain crops, and meadow. Bird species include puddle ducks, woodcocks, jack snipes, sora and Virginia rails, plovers, herons, and bitterns.

Viewing Information: This area's extensive system of dikes makes excellent elevated trails for viewing wetland wildlife such as great blue herons, great egrets, wood ducks, teal, frogs, muskrats, turtles, and dragonflies. Approximately half the area borders river habitat, and you can see open-water birds along these stretches. Little Portage Wildlife Area is open to hunters during regular hunting seasons.

Directions: From Port Clinton, follow State Route 53 south approximately 6 miles to Darr-Hopfinger Road. Take Darr-Hopfinger Road west approximately 2 miles to the area entrance.

Ownership: DOW, call 1-800-WILDLIFE for a free area map

Size: 407 acres   **Closest Town:** Port Clinton

27. PICKEREL CREEK WILDLIFE AREA

Description: This premier Ohio wetland is a flagship project of the North American Waterfowl Management Plan to protect, restore, and enhance key wetland habitats in North America. More than 1,100 acres of critical wetlands have been restored here. Located on the southern shore of Sandusky Bay, the area supports a bald eagle nest and a large number of Eastern prairie white-fringed orchids, which are on both state and federal threatened species lists. Peak flowering occurs about the first of July. Ducks, geese, herons, egrets, gulls, and shorebirds abound.

Viewing Information: An observation tower along U.S. Route 6 on the southern edge of the area gives a good overview of the marsh. Eastern prairie white-fringed orchids grow along the eastern side of Township Road 256 in the field just north of the pond. Bald eagles are seen frequently; however, the eagle nest itself is in a protected zone not visible to the public. Pickerel Creek Wildlife Area is open to hunting during regular hunting seasons. Blue Heron Reserve, a 160-acre wildlife preserve owned by the Sandusky County Park District, is immediately south of the Pickerel Creek Wildlife Area along U.S. Route 6.

Directions: *Pickerel Creek is located 0.5 mile east of U.S. Route 6 and State Route 510 in Sandusky County.*

Ownership: DOW, call 1-800-WILDLIFE for a free area map

Size: 2,571 acres   **Closest Town:** Clyde

More numerous in Ohio during the winter months, black ducks are considered some of the wariest waterfowl. Most often confused in identification with the female mallard, black ducks are the same size as mallards but a more chocolate brown in color with silver undersides to their wings. RON KEIL

28. RESTHAVEN WILDLIFE AREA

Description: Numerous pond habitats and their wildlife characterize this area of northern Ohio. The proximity of ponds to roads makes a good driving tour. Resthaven is Ohio's largest prairie remnant. Approximately 100 acres of plants such as prairie small white ladyslipper, blazing star, prairie gray-headed coneflower, and prairie dock thrive here. The best time to see the prairie bloom is mid- to late summer.

Viewing Information: You can see turtles, frogs, snakes, dragonflies, muskrats, raccoons, wood ducks, Canada geese, and other water-loving wildlife practically anywhere at Resthaven. Migratory songbird numbers can be high in spring and fall. The greatest concentration of prairie plants is immediately east of Northwest Road across from the dog training area. Resthaven Wildlife Area is open to hunting during regular hunting seasons. In the nearby town of Castalia is a city pond where ducks and geese by the hundreds—sometimes thousands—flourish. The pond is at the intersection of Main Street and State Route 101.

Directions: Immediately northwest of Castalia on State Route 269.

Ownership: DOW, call 1-800-WILDLIFE for a free area map

Size: 2,272 acres   **Closest Town:** Castalia

Masters of camouflage, gray treefrogs can change their color from gray-green to a light pearl-gray depending on their background. These small arboreal frogs seldom leave the trees except during breeding season, when they congregate at nearby ponds. Their short, loud trill can be heard coming from woodlands during the warmer months, especially just before or after a summer rain.

GARY MESLAROS

49

Description: The elaborate gates at the entrance are all that remain of the original automobile entrance to nearby Cedar Point amusement park. The original road was washed out by Lake Erie storms years ago, but remnants serve as an ideal hiking trail through the preserve. This area contains some of the last wetlands and undeveloped shoreline in the Sandusky Bay region. It is also one of the last Ohio remnants of a forest-marsh-lake ecosystem. Habitats include: old field, hardwood forest, woodland swamp, cattail marsh, barrier sand beach, and open lake. Nearly 300 bird species have been identified. It is also an important fledging area for bald eagles.

Viewing Information: Immediately north of the parking area is a field managed for monarch butterflies. Best viewing is late summer or early fall. Farther north, a shallow, 1-acre pond offers views of turtles and birds such as green-backed herons, ring-necked ducks, and occasional sora rails. The trail leads through hardwood forest where colorful wood warblers rest and feed during spring and fall migrations. April through June, view an explosion of wildflowers. Spectacular cardinal flowers bloom in the woodland swamps in summer. Farther along the trail, an observation deck overlooks the marsh, an excellent place to set up a spotting scope to observe shorebird and waterfowl migrations. Blanding's, midland painted, and snapping turtles bask here during warmer months. Endangered common terns nest on the mile-long barrier beach.

Directions: *From Huron, 1 mile west on U.S. Route 6. The entrance is on the north side of the road.*

Ownership: DNAP (419) 433-4919

Size: 463 acres   **Closest Town:** Huron

White-tailed deer reached their lowest numbers in Ohio about a century ago. Today, the Ohio deer herd has rebounded tremendously and is estimated at about half a million.

30. OLD WOMAN CREEK NATIONAL ESTUARINE RESEARCH RESERVE AND STATE NATURE PRESERVE

Description: This site on the south shore of Lake Erie just east of Huron is the only nationally designated freshwater estuary in the United States. It attracts not only abundant and varied wildlife, but also scientists and students from around the world. The area is a combination of estuarine wetland, open water, barrier sand beach, upland forest, and old field wildlife habitats.

Viewing Information: A paved, 0.25-mile, barrier-free trail leads from the visitor center parking lot through woods to an observation deck overlooking the estuary. A bald eagle nest is visible from this location when surrounding trees are bare. Other wildlife includes egrets, herons, grebes, rails, coots, wood ducks, ruddy ducks, buffleheads, loons, ospreys, muskrats, raccoons, and bats. Huge beds of American lotus bloom in summer. From the observation deck, trails and an elevated boardwalk lead through swamp-forest, upland hardwoods, and old fields. A second parking area immediately west of the bridge on U.S. Route 6 provides access to the barrier beach. During spring and fall migrations, waterfowl rafts composed of thousands of birds float on Lake Erie. Look for red-breasted mergansers, scaup, redheads, ring-necked ducks, canvasbacks, and other diving ducks. Many sandpipers, herons, and gulls occupy the beach in warmer weather.

Directions: *From Huron, follow U.S. Route 6 for 3 miles east.*

Ownership: DNAP (419) 433-4601

Size: 572 acres   **Closest Town:** Huron

Located along the Lake Erie shoreline just east of Huron, Old Woman Creek is the only nationally designated freshwater estuary in the United States, attracting not only wild animals, but scientists, students, and wildlife watchers from around the world. A visit any time of year will produce numerous wildlife sightings, mainly bird life.

GARY MESLAROS

DISTRICT THREE: NORTHEAST OHIO

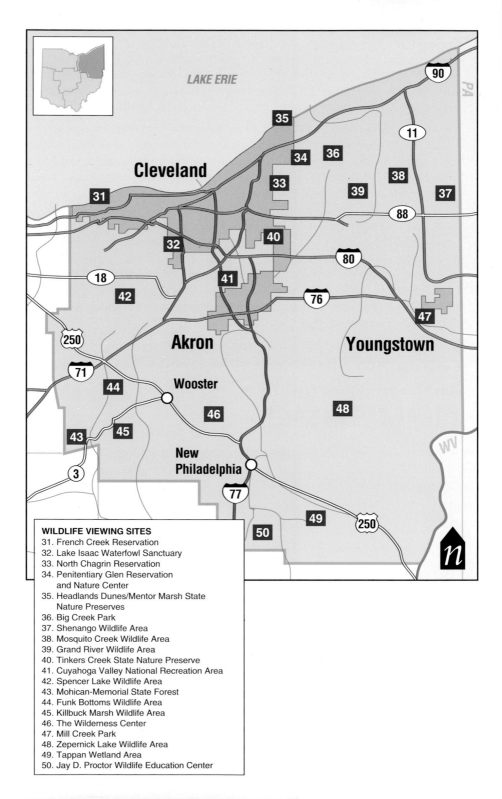

LAKE ERIE

Cleveland

Akron

Wooster

New Philadelphia

Youngstown

PA

WV

WILDLIFE VIEWING SITES
31. French Creek Reservation
32. Lake Isaac Waterfowl Sanctuary
33. North Chagrin Reservation
34. Penitentiary Glen Reservation
    and Nature Center
35. Headlands Dunes/Mentor Marsh State
    Nature Preserves
36. Big Creek Park
37. Shenango Wildlife Area
38. Mosquito Creek Wildlife Area
39. Grand River Wildlife Area
40. Tinkers Creek State Nature Preserve
41. Cuyahoga Valley National Recreation Area
42. Spencer Lake Wildlife Area
43. Mohican-Memorial State Forest
44. Funk Bottoms Wildlife Area
45. Killbuck Marsh Wildlife Area
46. The Wilderness Center
47. Mill Creek Park
48. Zepernick Lake Wildlife Area
49. Tappan Wetland Area
50. Jay D. Proctor Wildlife Education Center

31. FRENCH CREEK RESERVATION

Description: Woodland and brushland interspersed with wetlands and scenic ravines characterize this site. Fish and Sugar creeks cut deeply into underlying bedrock before joining larger French Creek and eventually the Black River. Nesting birds include wood thrushes and robins. Other birds are visible from the trails and the viewing windows that overlook feeding stations at the nature center. Also worth a visit is nearby Black River Reservation a few miles west.

Viewing Information: More than 4.5 miles of hiking trails lead through woodlands, across bridges and stairways, and along streams and cliffs. Stream species such as frogs, minnows, and raccoons are common. Woodland species include white-tailed deer, various hawks and owls, and small mammals.

Directions: From Interstate 90 east of Lorain, take State Route 611 approximately 2 miles west to the entrance.

Ownership: Lorain County Metroparks 1-800-LCM-PARK

Size: 428 acres   **Closest Town:** Lorain

32. LAKE ISAAC WATERFOWL SANCTUARY

Description: This small glacial kettle lake, one of the few remaining in the greater Cleveland area, lies in urban Middleburg Heights. Spring, and then autumn, are the best times to view wildlife. A short hiking trail around the northern side of the lake passes through a marsh, a floodplain, a pine plantation, woodlands, and an old orchard.

Viewing Information: The parking area immediately adjacent to the lake provides the best view of water birds. Canada geese, mallards, black ducks, wood ducks, and other waterfowl appear during peak migrations—March through April and October through November. Along the walking trail, you might see groundhogs, squirrels, opossums, skunks, white-tailed deer, or maybe a fox. Birds include blue-winged warblers, white-eyed vireos, warbling vireos, rose-breasted grosbeaks, Northern orioles, brown thrashers, tree swallows, wood ducks, and woodcocks.

Directions: From Interstate 71, take State Route 42 north (in Middleburg Heights) to Fowles Road. Go west on Fowles Road to Big Creek Parkway. Turn south on Big Creek Parkway and the parking area is 0.15 mile on the right.

Ownership: Cleveland Metroparks (216) 351-6300

Size: 100 acres   **Closest Town:** Middleburg Heights

33. NORTH CHAGRIN RESERVATION

Description: The highlights of this Cleveland Metropark just east of Cleveland are a 2-acre pond and 2-acre marsh. The large nature center houses interpretive displays, exhibits, a bookshop, and viewing windows that overlook the pond, marsh, and bird feeders. Within this site is A. B. Williams Memorial Woods, where huge beech and maple trees thrive. This woodland is listed on the National Registry of Natural Landmarks. Songbirds flourish in this climax forest, and squirrels, both fox and gray, are common. Enjoy scenic overlooks from the trails.

Viewing Information: A 2-story viewing tower beside Sunset Pond affords wildlife watchers a look at Canada geese, mallards, black ducks, wood ducks, and herons. Adjacent Sanctuary Marsh has a 300-foot-long boardwalk and viewing deck built over the water. From the boardwalk you can see painted turtles, snapping turtles, Northern water snakes, bullfrogs, and green frogs sunning themselves during the warmer months. Water birds are common. Fish such as bluegills, sunfish, largemouth bass, and crappies are visible from the boardwalk. The surrounding woods provide habitat for birds of prey such as red-shouldered hawks and barred and screech owls. Aquatic mammals include muskrats, raccoons, mink, and beaver.

Directions: *From Interstate 271 east of Cleveland, take Wilson Mills Road approximately 0.5 mile east to State Route 91 (SOM Center Road). Turn north and follow SOM Center Road 2.5 miles to the park entrance on the east side of the road. Once in the park, turn right at the first stop sign. The entrance to Sunset Wildlife Preserve is 0.5 mile on the right.*

Ownership: Cleveland Metroparks (216) 351-6300

Size: 1,900 acres   **Closest Town:** Mayfield Village

Peregrine falcons, who use cliff ledges as nesting platforms in the wild, have adapted to nesting on building ledges in Ohio and now nest in the cities of Cincinnati, Cleveland, Columbus, Dayton, and Toledo.

34. PENITENTIARY GLEN RESERVATION AND NATURE CENTER

Description: A small, clear stream running through a beautiful, hemlock-lined gorge distinguishes this northeastern Ohio site. The name alludes to the 90-foot walls of the gorge, or glen: easy access, tough exit—much like a penitentiary. The area's newly renovated nature center is surrounded by a 2,400-square-foot butterfly-hummingbird garden, a small pond, and a marsh. Birds of prey and other wildlife undergoing rehabilitation are on display at the Wildlife Center.

Viewing Information: Five trails (some paved) through field, forest, pond, and marsh offer viewing opportunities. Songbirds are common, as are fox squirrels, white-tailed deer, and chipmunks. The gorge is a unique and fragile community sheltering unusual plants such as mountain maple and trailing arbutus. The nature center houses interactive displays, a working honeybee hive, aquariums, a viewing window, and gift shop. Scheduled during the summer is a miniature steam engine that pulls carloads of visitors through the woodlands along the gorge rim. Stoney Brook Falls is worth the walk.

Directions: From Cleveland, follow Interstate 90 east to State Route 306 (Mentor/Kirtland exit). Proceed south on State Route 306 0.5 mile to Kirtland-Chardon Road. Take Kirtland-Chardon Road 2 miles to the park entrance.

Ownership: Lake Metroparks (216) 256-1404

Size: 380 acres   **Closest Town:** Kirtland City

The largest of four tree squirrel species in Ohio, fox squirrels can be found statewide. They did not originally inhabit Ohio's virgin forests; it was only as timber was cut and land cleared that they extended their range from the Midwest prairie edges into the state. Today, they are most common in the woodlot country of agricultural western Ohio. L. WEST

55

35. HEADLANDS DUNES AND MENTOR MARSH STATE NATURE PRESERVES

Description: These unique sites in northeastern Ohio lie within a stone's throw of each other. Headlands Dunes, on the shores of Lake Erie, is one of the last sand dune-beach communities in Ohio and is the northern terminus of the state-spanning Buckeye Trail. Atlantic Coastal Plain plant species such as sea rocket, beach pea, seaside spurge, beach grass, and purple sand grass grow on the dunes. Mentor Marsh, immediately southwest of Headlands Dunes, occupies the ancient riverbed of the Grand River. Phragmites, or reedgrass, grows to heights of 12 feet and covers much of the marsh.

Viewing Information: A refreshing walk along the Lake Erie shoreline at Headlands Dunes offers a good opportunity to see waterfowl, gulls, sandpipers, and other shorebirds. The preserve is adjacent to Fairport Harbor; during storms, birds rest in the calm waters behind the break wall. Fairport lighthouse, at the end of the break wall, is a popular photo subject. Mentor Marsh is a birding hot spot with more than 250 species recorded. It is not unusual for expert birders to hear or see 125 species or more per day during migrations.

Directions: *Headlands Dunes State Nature Preserve is located just west of Fairport Harbor at the north end of State Route 44 and the east end of Headlands Beach State Park. Mentor Marsh State Nature Preserve is located on the east edge of Mentor, 3.5 miles west of Painesville on State Route 283, then 0.5 mile north on Corduroy Road.*

Ownership: DNAP (216) 563-9344, and Cleveland Museum of Natural History

Size: Headlands Dunes, 24 acres; Mentor Marsh, 647 acres

Closest Town: Mentor

Although nearly extirpated from the entire Great Lakes region at the turn of the century by the millinery trade, ring-billed gulls are found in Ohio today by the thousands, both inland and along Lake Erie. These scavengers feed anywhere from lakes, dumps, and shopping center parking lots to cultivated fields. In late fall a flock of 100,000 or more gulls gathers along the Cleveland-Lorain lakefront.

MARK ROMESSER

36. BIG CREEK PARK

Description: Extensive beech-maple woods characterize this site. In spring, large-flowered trillium carpet the forest floor. Neotropical songbirds nest here: thrushes, tanagers, flycatchers, vireos, and several wood warblers. Hemlock ravines provide summer habitat for northern bird species such as dark-eyed juncos and winter wrens. The park contains three ponds, 12 hiking trails, and an excellent nature center.

Viewing Information: Big Creek Park offers year-round wildlife watching. Songbirds, hawks, owls, squirrels, white-tailed deer, and beaver inhabit the area. Instructive programs for all age groups enhance knowledge of amphibians, wildflowers, neotropical songbirds, and winter wildlife. You might want to combine this trip with a visit to the Walter C. Best Wildlife Preserve just south of Chardon on State Route 44. There, a 30-acre lake with viewing blind allows close observation of migratory waterfowl.

Directions: *From Chardon, follow North Street (Ravenna Road) from the village square north 1 mile to Woodin Road. Turn east on Woodin Road and follow it 1 mile to Robinson Road. Go north on Robinson 1 mile to the park entrance.*

Ownership: Geauga Park District (216) 285-2222, ext. 5420

Size: 642 acres   **Closest Town:** Chardon

37. SHENANGO WILDLIFE AREA

Description: This long, narrow site in northeastern Ohio lies along the Pennsylvania border and parallels most of Pymatuning Creek. Much of the habitat is beaver swamp, interspersed with upland fields and woodlands. Waterfowl, furbearers, and songbirds are abundant. Shenango is an excellent place to watch woodcock mating flights at dawn and dusk during spring.

Viewing Information: Start your tour at the 40-acre wetland at the end of Milligan Road, on the southern end of the area. To get there, drive west on Milligan from Orangeville-Kinsman Road to the first parking area south of the road. Then walk west along the road approximately 200 yards. During warmer months, you'll see swallows, belted kingfishers, great blue herons, ducks, geese, turtles, frogs, dragonflies, and muskrats. Or explore Shenango by canoe down Pymatuning Creek. Shenango is open to hunting during regular hunting seasons.

Directions: *From Vernon Center, the wildlife area lies immediately east of State Route 7.*

Ownership: DOW, call 1-800-WILDLIFE for a free area map

Size: 4,845 acres   **Closest Town:** Vernon Center

38. MOSQUITO CREEK WILDLIFE AREA

Description: This large site in northeastern Ohio encompasses the northern end of Mosquito Lake and is managed primarily for waterfowl. Much of the area is a waterfowl refuge closed to hiking, but plenty of wildlife is visible from the roads, including a resident flock of nearly 2,000 Canada geese. During spring and fall migrations, the count increases to as many as 13,000 honkers. Ducks are plentiful; most common are wood ducks, mallards, teal, scaup, and black ducks. Several hundred tundra swans stop by during migrations.

Viewing Information: Pintail Pond and Mallard Pond, along Township Road 240 on the southern edge of the area, are good places to see waterfowl, especially in spring and fall. The eastern end of Township Road 240 overlooks Mosquito Lake, where you'll see shorebirds such as killdeer on the mud flats. Occasionally, bald eagles are visible at the large wetland on either side of County Road 263 a mile south of headquarters. Portions of the area are open to hunting during regular hunting seasons.

Directions: *From Cortland, follow State Route 46 approximately 8 miles north to State Route 87. Turn west and follow State Route 87 1 mile to Greene Center. Mosquito Creek Wildlife Area lies immediately south of State Route 87 between Greene Center and North Bloomfield.*

Ownership: DOW, call 1-800-WILDLIFE for a free area map

Size: 8,525 acres   **Closest Town:** Cortland

Once nearly gone from the state, Canada geese are now seen in Ohio by the thousands. Two subspecies frequent the state: Giant Canada geese nest here and tend to stay year-round. The Southern James Bay population of Canada geese are the ones seen migrating through Ohio spring and fall. GARY MESLAROS

39. GRAND RIVER WILDLIFE AREA

Description: Extensive swamp-forest, once typical of much of northeastern Ohio, characterizes the site. This portion of the Grand River valley is one of the largest semi-wilderness areas remaining in this part of the state. The 12 ponds, numerous beaver impoundments, and 12 man-made marshes make good habitat for river otters. These fascinating creatures, once extirpated from Ohio, were reintroduced to the state at the Grand River Wildlife Area during winter 1986-87, and again in spring 1988. Reproduction has been documented, and young otters have been observed.

Viewing Information: Begin your tour at the large wetland 0.25 mile west of County Road 213 on the southern part of the area. From State Route 88, follow C-213 south 0.5 mile to a parking area east of the road. Across the road, opposite the parking area, is a gravel trail offering a level, easy 5-minute walk to the wetland. A boardwalk spanning the wetland allows you to view beaver activity: gnawed stumps, drowned trees, and a beaver lodge. Other wildlife includes waterfowl, shorebirds, and muskrats. Songbirds are abundant in the surrounding swamp-forest. Grand River Wildlife Area is open to hunting during regular hunting seasons.

Directions: *From West Farmington, follow State Route 88 for 1 mile east to State Route 534. The Grand River Wildlife Area lies both north and south of State Route 88, and immediately east of State Route 534.*

Ownership: DOW, call 1-800-WILDLIFE for a free area map

Size: 6,799 acres   **Closest Town:** West Farmington

NORTHEAST OHIO

Lake Erie is known as the "Walleye Capital of the World," where millions of walleyes are caught from Ohio waters each year.

40. TINKERS CREEK STATE NATURE PRESERVE

Description: An extensive marsh occupies approximately three-fourths of this site. Several spring-fed, man-made ponds are scattered through bottomlands of swamp white oak and pin oak. Canada geese, mallards, and wood ducks nest throughout the marsh. Beavers, white-tailed deer, raccoons, mink, weasels, muskrats, and foxes frequent the area. Reptiles and amphibians include snapping turtles, water snakes, four-toed salamanders, and bullfrogs. A large heronry of 80 or more nests is another highlight.

Viewing Information: The 1.5-mile Seven Ponds Trail offers excellent birding. Songbirds, geese, and herons are usually visible, especially from the viewing platform. South Point Trail flashes with colorful wood warblers in mid-May. From the terminus of this trail visitors can see beaver ponds and marsh to the south and west. Beaver activity is apparent around Lonesome Pond. Tinkers Creek State Park is nearby.

Directions: From Aurora, follow Hudson-Aurora Road 1.5 miles southwest, then turn west on Old Mill Road and go 1.5 miles to the area entrance adjacent to the railroad tracks.

Ownership: DNAP (216) 527-5118

Size: 786 acres   **Closest Town:** Aurora

A visit to Tinkers Creek is always worthwhile, but spring and fall are best for peak migratory wildlife activity. Mid-May is the time to see colorful wood warblers. November marks the peak of the waterfowl migration. Canada geese are present year-round, except when the ponds are frozen in winter. JIM ROETZEL

Description: The marsh near the Ira Trailhead of the Ohio & Erie Canal Towpath Trail is a prime example of a wetland habitat created by beavers. An easy 10-minute walk to the marsh takes you along remnants of the Ohio & Erie Canal, including Lock #26 and a wayside exhibit describing its past. A boardwalk with viewing platform spans the marsh. Beavers, amphibians, songbirds, and aquatic plants are the most notable attractions. The entire 33,000 acres, with hiking trails, bike paths, and picnic and recreation areas, offers excellent birding.

Viewing Information: On your way from the trailhead parking lot north to the beaver marsh, look for songbirds and wildflowers during warm months. You might see unusual summer birds such as black-billed cuckoos and scarlet tanagers along this stretch. During winter, listen for song sparrows and a variety of woodpeckers. When you get to the boardwalk, look for water birds such as wood ducks, great blue herons, green herons, and belted kingfishers. If you are out at dawn or dusk, watch for muskrats, beavers, raccoons, and bats, and listen to the chorus of green, tree, and bullfrogs.

Directions: *From Interstate 77 south of Cleveland, take the Wheatley Road/ Richfield exit (exit 143). Follow Wheatley Road 4.8 miles east to Riverview Road. Turn south on Riverview Road and go 1.5 miles to the Ira Trailhead. Hike or bike 0.33 mile north on the Ohio & Erie Canal Towpath Trail to the beaver marsh.*

Ownership: NPS (216) 524-1497

Size: 33,000 acres   **Closest Town:** Cuyahoga Falls

NORTHEAST OHIO

Forest wildlife habitat, which once covered 95 percent of Ohio, dipped to a low of 10 percent a century ago. It has now recovered to 30 percent and is increasing.

42. SPENCER LAKE WILDLIFE AREA

Description: This small wildlife area in northeastern Ohio boasts varied wild-life habitats: woodland, cropland, lake, old field, grassland, brushland, marsh, and river. A great variety of nesting and migrant birds use the area; of particular interest is the spring migration of waterfowl and songbirds. Cottontail rabbits, fox squirrels, muskrats, raccoons, mink, opossum, and skunks are common, with occasional white-tailed deer.

Viewing Information: A causeway divides the lake, and the fishing/viewing platforms on either side are good places from which to see waterfowl, shore-birds, and other wetland wildlife. Surrounding the lake are upland habitats and marshland that attract songbirds and game birds. The meandering Black River is the western boundary of the area. Spencer Lake Wildlife Area is open to hunting during the regular hunting seasons.

Directions: From Spencer, follow State Route 162 east approximately 3 miles.

Ownership: DOW, call 1-800-WILDLIFE for a free area map

Size: 618 acres   **Closest Town:** Spencer

43. MOHICAN-MEMORIAL STATE FOREST

Description: This state forest and adjacent Mohican State Park lie on the western edge of unglaciated northeastern Ohio. Within the forest, Clear Fork Gorge State Nature Preserve protects a natural stand of mature white pines. The beautiful, hemlock-lined Clear Fork Gorge itself is on the National Registry of Natural Landmarks as designated by the National Park Service. The Clear Fork of the Mohican River runs through the forest and offers one of the few trout fishing opportunities in Ohio. A fire tower gives an overview of surrounding woodland habitat.

Viewing Information: Mohican is an excellent place to see neotropical migrant songbirds. Watch and listen for wild turkeys, too. A 1-mile hike upstream from the covered bridge through the gorge to the top of Pleasant Hill Dam offers a spectacular view of Pleasant Hill Lake. A side trip along this route takes you to Big Lyons and Little Lyons falls. Turkey vultures and red-tailed hawks soar above the gorge. White-tailed deer, gray squirrels, and chipmunks are plentiful. Black rat snakes, box turtles, and salamanders are common during warmer months. Mohican-Memorial State Forest (excluding Memorial Forest Park) is open to hunting during the regular hunting seasons.

Directions: From Loudonville, follow State Route 3 approximately 2 miles south to State Route 97. Mohican-Memorial State Forest lies along State Route 97, west of State Route 3.

Ownership: DOF (419) 938-6222

Size: 4,506 acres   **Closest Town:** Loudonville

44. FUNK BOTTOMS WILDLIFE AREA

Description: Visit this area in spring, when the moist-soil meadows and bottomland hardwoods are flooded, creating a major attraction for birds; 23 waterfowl species (including tundra swans) and 28 shorebird species have been recorded. Several raptor species appear during migrations; some spend the winter. Bald eagles have been observed, and barn owls utilize nest boxes. Sandhill cranes, an endangered species in Ohio, were confirmed to be nesting here in 1988—the first nesting of this species recorded in Ohio in more than 60 years! Sandhill nests have been documented several times since.

Viewing Information: The best views of waterfowl and shorebirds are south of State Route 95 immediately southeast of Funk. Songbirds are abundant along the Jerome Fork 1 mile west of Funk. Wildlife common to the area include: mallards, wood ducks, Canada geese, muskrats, raccoons, cottontail rabbits, white-tailed deer, ring-necked pheasants, groundhogs, and fox squirrels. Funk Bottoms Wildlife Area is open to hunting during regular hunting seasons.

Directions: From Funk, immediately southeast along State Route 95, or 1 mile west along State Route 95.

Ownership: DOW, call 1-800-WILDLIFE for a free area map

Size: 1,154 acres   **Closest Town:** Funk

The most prolific furbearers in Ohio, muskrats live in virtually every wetland area in the state. In swamps and marshes their conical houses of mud and vegetation are built six to eight feet wide and two to four feet tall. Along rivers, streams, and ponds they will forgo building a house in favor of a bank den burrowed into the shore, the entrance usually underwater. Muskrat droppings on rocks along waterways are evidence of their nocturnal activities. IAN ADAMS

NORTHEAST OHIO

45. KILLBUCK MARSH WILDLIFE AREA

Description: This site near the heart of Amish country boasts the largest inland marsh in Ohio. Killbuck is also one of the few places in the state where sandhill cranes nest and rear young. River otters, endangered in Ohio, were released on the area in 1991. A 5-mile wildlife observation trail is being established on the abandoned railroad bed through the center of the marsh. When completed, it will pass through a variety of habitats. Wetland species abound.

Viewing Information: This area makes a good auto tour—some roads are adjacent to marsh or swamp and much wildlife is visible from a vehicle. Killbuck is also excellent for canoeing and boating to observe the marsh more closely. Water birds are abundant: wood ducks, geese, herons, belted kingfishers, swallows, and rails. Mammals include beavers, muskrats, white-tailed deer, cottontail rabbits, groundhogs, fox squirrels, skunks, and raccoons. Also plentiful are frogs, fish, and turtles. The Eastern massasauga, a small wetland rattlesnake, has been reported here. Killbuck Marsh Wildlife Area is open to hunting during regular hunting seasons.

Directions: *From Wooster, follow State Route 83 approximately 4 miles south.*

Ownership: DOW, call 1-800-WILDLIFE for a free area map

Size: 5,492 acres   **Closest Town:** Wooster

Wood ducks are the most abundant nesting waterfowl in the state, preferring hollow trees as nest sites. These tree cavities can be as high as 65 feet above the ground, although about half that height is average. When young wood ducks are first hatched they are flightless and must jump to the ground from the nest. Landing uninjured, the young ducklings are quickly led to the nearest water by their mother.
BRADY KOLDEN

46. THE WILDERNESS CENTER

Description: Located in the rolling hills of northeastern Ohio's Amish country, this area features hiking trails through mature woods, reverting farm fields, marsh, lake, pond, and prairie. Wildlife viewing windows in the large interpretive building look out on bird and animal feeders. A unique fish viewing pavilion at the lake makes an interesting stop. Two tallgrass prairies bloom mid-summer through fall. Sigrist Woods, a virgin stand of mammoth beech, maple, and oak, is listed as an Ohio Natural Landmark.

Viewing Information: From the pavilion over the water at Wilderness Lake, watch bluegill, sunfish, and bass. An observation tower along the pond trail gives a treetop view of surrounding hardwood forest. Songbirds, small mammals, and white-tailed deer are abundant. The trails are open dawn to dusk daily. The interpretive building is open Tuesday through Saturday, 9 a.m. to 5 p.m., and Sunday 1 p.m. to 5 p.m., closed on Monday.

Directions: *From Wilmot, follow U.S. Route 250 approximately 1 mile west to Alabama Avenue. Turn north, and the entrance is approximately 0.5 mile on the left.*

Ownership: The Wilderness Center Membership (330) 359-5235

Size: 573 acres **Closest Town:** Wilmot

47. MILL CREEK PARK

Description: The northern half of this large urban park on the west side of Youngstown includes Mill Creek Gorge, characterized by sandstone outcroppings on steep hillsides of deciduous and evergreen trees. The southern half is comparatively flat, consisting of dense woods and extensive swamps. Twenty-one miles of roads and 15 miles of trails offer birding and other wildlife viewing.

Viewing Information: Three lakes surrounded by mature forest in the center of Mill Creek Park attract wetland and woodland wildlife, including beavers and white-tailed deer. Waterfowl, frogs, and turtles flourish at 70-acre Lake Newport, 44-acre Lake Glacier, and 28-acre Lake Cohasset. The Lily Pond is also rich in aquatic life. Visit the nature center on Old Furnace Road.

Directions: *Located on the west side of Youngstown between State Route 224 to the south and Interstate 680 to the north.*

Ownership: Mill Creek Metropolitan Park District (330) 702-3000

Size: 2,530 acres **Closest Town:** Youngstown

48. ZEPERNICK LAKE WILDLIFE AREA

Description: This small site in northeastern Ohio is worth a quick stop if you're in the vicinity. A 39-acre lake, three ponds, and a mixture of upland habitats attract waterfowl, songbirds, small mammals, reptiles, amphibians, fish, and insects.

Viewing Information: An elevated parking lot north of State Route 172 gives a good overview of the lake. A quarter mile west on the south side of State Route 172 is the entrance to the parking area for Ruff Pond. Zepernick Lake Wildlife Area is open to hunting during the regular hunting seasons.

Directions: *From Hanoverton, follow State Route 9 approximately 3 miles north to State Route 172. Turn west and follow it 3 miles to the area.*

Ownership: DOW, call 1-800-WILDLIFE for a free area map

Size: 513 acres   **Closest Town:** Hanoverton

49. TAPPAN WETLAND AREA

Description: This relatively small, remote wetland is surrounded by beautiful hills of mature oak-hickory forest. The combination attracts common Ohio wetland species, as well as white-tailed deer and wild turkeys. Red-tailed hawks and turkey vultures soar above ridges on afternoon thermals. Fall color can be exceptional.

Viewing Information: A wildlife observation deck overlooks two ponds and a small marsh. Nearby Tappan Lake cove attracts belted kingfishers, great blue herons, and waterfowl. One-mile Turkey Ridge Trail connects the wetland to 5,000-acre Tappan Lake Park. Birding along this trail can be productive, especially in spring. Watch for pileated woodpeckers, flickers, and songbirds such as white-throated sparrows.

Directions: *From State Route 250 just south of Tappan Lake, turn west on County Road 55 and follow it to County Road 2 (toward Deersville). At Beall Road, turn right and follow it until it dead ends at Tappan Wetland Area. (From State Route 250 it is approximately 4 miles.)*

Ownership: Muskingum Watershed Conservancy District, Tappan Lake Park (614) 922-3649

Size: 220 acres   **Closest Town:** Deersville

50. JAY D. PROCTOR WILDLIFE EDUCATION CENTER

Description: Beautiful, rolling hills of woodland, brushland, and old fields attract birds of field and forest. Raptors and bluebirds are common. Mammals include white-tailed deer, raccoons, groundhogs, skunks, opossums, weasels, mice, and shrews.

Viewing Information: School groups and conservation organizations may request guided birding tours by calling (614) 594-2211. Unlike other areas owned by the Ohio Division of Wildlife, this is a wildlife refuge and is not open to hunting.

Directions: *From Newcomerstown, follow State Route 258 approximately 7 miles southeast to Postboy Road. Turn west and follow Postboy Road to the entrance.*

Ownership: DOW, call 1-800-WILDLIFE for a free area map

Size: 256 acres   **Closest Town:** Newcomerstown

Eastern bluebirds were abundant in Ohio during the early part of the 20th century, when most of the state was a mosaic of small farms made up of fields of hay, oats, corn, pastures, and orchards—ideal bluebird habitat. But as farming evolved toward larger fields of corn and soybeans and away from pastures and orchards, much bluebird habitat was lost. Today, the Eastern bluebird is on the rebound partly because of its ready use of man-made nest boxes. Free plans for bluebird nest boxes are available from the Ohio Division of Wildlife. Call 1-800-WILDLIFE and ask for publication 339, "Hit the Trail for Bluebirds."

RON AUSTING

DISTRICT FOUR: SOUTHEAST OHIO

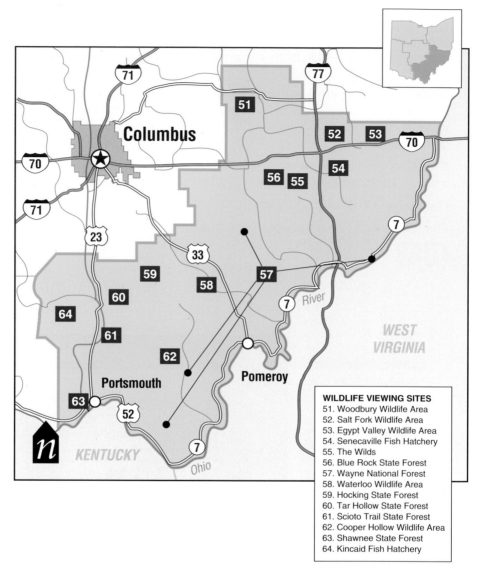

WILDLIFE VIEWING SITES
51. Woodbury Wildlife Area
52. Salt Fork Wildlife Area
53. Egypt Valley Wildlife Area
54. Senecaville Fish Hatchery
55. The Wilds
56. Blue Rock State Forest
57. Wayne National Forest
58. Waterloo Wildlife Area
59. Hocking State Forest
60. Tar Hollow State Forest
61. Scioto Trail State Forest
62. Cooper Hollow Wildlife Area
63. Shawnee State Forest
64. Kincaid Fish Hatchery

51. WOODBURY WILDLIFE AREA

Description: Extensive grassland and brushland, the result of surface coal mine reclamation, typify Ohio's largest wildlife area. Birds of prey are abundant, and uncommon species such as short-eared owls and rough-legged hawks reside here in winter. Numerous small wetlands in the valleys attract waterfowl and shorebirds. Coyote populations are increasing in Ohio; take advantage of expansive views to possibly get a look at this adaptable predator.

Viewing Information: Numerous roads provide ample opportunity to see wildlife from a vehicle. You're likely to see evidence of beavers: beaver dams and beaver lodges. Woodbury is a wild turkey management area. These wily birds are easiest to spot in late winter; listen for gobbling during April. Woodbury is open to hunting during the regular hunting seasons.

Directions: *This huge area lies approximately 5 miles west of Coshocton, both north and south of State Route 541.*

Ownership: DOW, call 1-800-WILDLIFE for a free area map

Size: 19,049 acres   **Closest Town:** Coshocton

The return of the wild turkey is a true wildlife management success story, not only in Ohio but nationally as well. These big birds were extirpated from the state at the turn of the century. The Ohio Division of Wildlife began reintroduction of this species in the late 1950s and early 1960s. Today, the Ohio wild turkey flock is estimated at well over 100,000 birds and increasing rapidly.

SCOTTY LOVETT

SOUTHEAST OHIO

52. SALT FORK WILDLIFE AREA

Description: This large viewing site in eastern Ohio is adjacent to Salt Fork Lake and Salt Fork State Park. Terrain is steep to rolling. Oak-hickory woods mark the ridges, and small streams dissect the valleys. Numerous beaver dams and ponds dot the area. Salt Fork is a great place to see white-tailed deer, especially in winter. Wild turkeys gobble from the ridgetops in spring. Autumn colors can be exceptional. A beautiful lodge at the state park invites overnight guests.

Viewing Information: Begin your visit at the 80-acre marsh on the extreme eastern end, where you might see wood ducks, wading birds, and shorebirds. View white-tailed deer feeding at dusk along Road 1, the main entrance to Salt Fork State Park off U.S. Route 22. Watch for open-water birds and waterfowl along Salt Fork Lake's 74 miles of shoreline and coves. Salt Fork Wildlife Area is open to hunting during regular hunting seasons.

Directions: From Cambridge, follow U.S. Route 22 approximately 7 miles east.

Ownership: DOW, call 1-800-WILDLIFE for a free area map

Size: 8,086 acres   **Closest Town:** Cambridge

According to the U.S. Fish and Wildlife Service, 76 million Americans now enjoy watching wildlife, and 30 million of those people regularly take trips away from home to view wildlife. Wildlife watching as a recreational activity has increased 63 percent over the last decade.

Description: The second largest wildlife area in Ohio takes its name from the second largest excavating machine in the world, the Gem of Egypt, once used to remove coal from surrounding hills. The extensive grasslands are reclaimed surface mines. Other habitats include woodland, brushland, pond, marsh, and stream. River otters recently released near Egypt Valley Wildlife Area have become established.

Viewing Information: Grassland species include wintering short-eared owls and other raptors as well as game birds, meadowlarks, and small mammals. Numerous ponds draw wading and shorebirds. White-tailed deer feed at dawn and dusk. Egypt Valley Wildlife Area is open to hunting during regular hunting seasons.

Directions: The area consists of two large parcels located north of the intersection of Interstate 70 and State Route 800. The east parcel lies between State Route 331 and Piedmont Lake. The west parcel lies between State Route 800 and Piedmont Lake.

Ownership: DOW, call 1-800-WILDLIFE for a free area map

Size: 14,300 acres   **Closest Town:** Morristown

SOUTHEAST OHIO

Distinctive and conspicuous, bobolinks are grassland birds, numerous in the many acres of reclaimed strip mine lands at Egypt Valley Wildlife Area. Brightly colored males, perched on weed stalks, defend their territories with a loud, bubbly song. These birds did not begin moving into Ohio until the 19th century, as the original forests were cleared. By 1900 they were considered common summer residents, and their numbers continued to increase during the next few decades. Populations peaked during the mid-20th century and then began a gradual decline as grassland was converted to crop fields. Today, bobolinks are found mostly in the glaciated part of the state. Bobolinks are members of the blackbird family. MARIE READ

54. SENECAVILLE FISH HATCHERY

Description: Three to 5 million fish are raised here annually. Species include walleye, saugeye, striped bass, hybrid striped bass, and channel catfish. The public is welcome 8 a.m. to 4:30 p.m. Thirty-seven outdoor rearing ponds attract varied wildlife.

Viewing Information: Great blue herons, yellowlegs, and ospreys feed here. Furbearers such as muskrats and raccoons are common at dawn and dusk. The hatchery is a stone's throw from Seneca Lake and its waterfowl; Seneca Lake Park draws songbirds and small mammals. White-tailed deer roam the surrounding forest.

Directions: *From Interstate 77 south of Cambridge, follow State Route 313 approximately 5 miles east to State Route 574. Turn south and go 0.33 mile to the hatchery entrance.*

Ownership: DOW (614) 685-5541

Size: 117 acres   **Closest Town:** Senecaville

55. THE WILDS (INTERNATIONAL CENTER FOR THE PRESERVATION OF WILD ANIMALS)

Description: This is North America's largest wildlife conservation and research center. Surface coal mines have been reclaimed to rolling, grassy rangeland resembling African savannah. Watch for native Ohio species such as dickcissels, bobolinks, harriers, short-eared owls, trumpeter swans, Canada geese, ducks, and white-tailed deer. You can also see rare and endangered African and Asian species such as zebra, antelope, oryx, eland, gazelle, hartebeest, giraffe, rhinoceros, kob, camel, wild horse, deer, and crane.

Viewing Information: The entrance fee is discounted to schools and groups. For no-cost views of native wildlife, drive the perimeter roads. Try Zion Ridge Road or State Route 284 on the west, International Road on the south, and State Route 340 on the east. The visitor center offers beautiful, panoramic views.

Directions: *From Cumberland, follow State Route 340 approximately 3 miles south to International Road. Turn west on International Road and proceed 0.5 mile to the Wilds entrance.*

Ownership: International Center for the Preservation of Wild Animals/the Wilds (614) 638-5030

Size: 9,154 acres   **Closest Town:** Cumberland

56. BLUE ROCK STATE FOREST

Description: Rugged, wooded hills shelter white-tailed deer, wild turkeys, and forest songbirds. Fall colors can be spectacular, and seeing them from horseback along the many bridle trails is especially rewarding. Keen-eyed observers might see salamanders of several species. The forest is adjacent to Blue Rock State Park.

Viewing Information: Browning Road is a must for a driving tour. A fire tower along Ridgeview Road gives a good overview of the forest. For more wildlife viewing information, stop by the forest headquarters along Cutler Lake Road. Blue Rock State Forest is open to hunting during regular hunting seasons.

Directions: From Duncan Falls, follow State Route 60 approximately 0.5 mile south to Cutler Lake Road (County Road 45), then turn east about 2 miles to the forest office.

Ownership: DOF (614) 674-4035

Size: 4,579 acres   **Closest Town:** Duncan Falls

Copperheads have the dubious distinction of having bitten more people in the United States than any other poisonous snake. The bite is rarely fatal, yet extremely painful. Their coloration not only acts as excellent camouflage, but also makes them one of the state's most beautiful reptiles. Copperheads are widely scattered throughout most of unglaciated Ohio. And although they inhabit a variety of habitats from floodplains to ridgetops, they prefer the rocky, wooded hillsides of southeastern Ohio. The state's two other poisonous snakes are the timber rattlesnake and the Eastern massasauga, also known as the swamp rattlesnake. GARY MESLAROS

57. WAYNE NATIONAL FOREST

Description: Ohio's only national forest, "The Wayne" is divided into three main sections and sprawls over more than 220,000 acres in the southeastern part of the state. As expected, woodland wildlife habitat is most abundant, but the forest boundaries also encompass many acres of upland and some wetland habitats. White-tailed deer, wild turkeys, forest songbirds, birds of prey, and numerous species of reptiles and amphibians inhabit various locations.

Viewing Information: For those wishing to hike and see woodland wildlife, try Wildcat Hollow Backpack Trail (15 miles) near Corning, or Symmes Creek Trail (6 miles) near Gallipolis. If you're looking for less strenuous viewing, try the Lake Vesuvius area near Ironton. To see wetland wildlife, the Leith Run Recreation Area near Newport has two observation decks, one offering a view of the Ohio River and the other overlooking the backwaters of Leith Run. Portions of Wayne National Forest are open to hunting during the regular hunting seasons.

Directions: *Wildcat Hollow Trailhead: (Athens District) From Corning, follow State Route 13 south 3.7 miles and then turn east onto Perry County Road 16 and follow signs to trailhead.*

Symmes Creek Trailhead: (Ironton District) From the intersection of State Routes 141 and 233, travel east 0.5 mile on State Route 141 and then follow signs to the trailhead using County Roads 12 and 15.

Lake Vesuvius: (Ironton District) From Ironton, follow State Route 93 approximately 8 miles north to County Road 29 and then east one mile to the area entrance.

Leith Run Recreation Area: (Marietta Unit, Fee Area) From Marietta, follow State Route 7 north approximately 20 miles to the area entrance.

Ownership: USFS, Athens Ranger District (614) 592-6644; Marietta Unit (614) 373-9055; Ironton Ranger District (614) 532-3223

Size: 221,000 acres   **Closest Town:** See viewing information

Black bears, once extirpated from Ohio, are beginning to return to the state. Populations are currently estimated at less than 100 bears. Sows with cubs have been reported, indicating that reproduction is possibly taking place in Ohio.

58. WATERLOO WILDLIFE AREA

Description: This area, combined with adjacent 26,380-acre Zaleski State Forest, is one of the largest parcels of woodland in Ohio. Waterloo is also the home of the Ohio Division of Wildlife's Forest Wildlife Research Station, where studies have been conducted for years on white-tailed deer, gray squirrels, ruffed grouse, wild turkeys, forest songbirds, and birds of prey. Another highlight is the many trees that are more than 100 years old, mainly oak-hickory on the narrow ridges and beech-maple in the deep ravines.

Viewing Information: Dozens of foot trails provide excellent access to these heavily forested hills, where some 80 species of birds have been recorded. Part of the area is a wild turkey management unit. Go eyeball-to-eyeball with turkey vultures and red-tailed hawks from the 90-foot fire tower. Views from here are especially beautiful during autumn. Waterloo is located just 7 miles from Lake Hope State Park. Waterloo Wildlife Area is open to hunting during regular hunting seasons.

Directions: *From Athens, follow State Route 56 approximately 10 miles west to the intersection of State Route 356.*

Ownership: DOW, call 1-800-WILDLIFE for a free area map

Size: 1,521 acres   **Closest Town:** Athens

59. HOCKING STATE FOREST

Description: Hocking State Forest is part of the Hocking Hills Region, considered by many to be the most beautiful area of the state. Steep, heavily wooded hillsides of oak-hickory forest hide waterfalls, massive rock outcroppings, and caves. Three state nature preserves (Conkles Hollow, Little Rocky Hollow, and Sheick Hollow) have been established within Hocking State Forest. Adjacent Hocking Hills State Park includes five areas: Ash Cave, Old Man's Cave, Rock House, Cedar Falls, and Cantwell Cliffs. These boast some of the most striking cliffs and land formations in Ohio. Forest wildlife abounds, and fall color can be spectacular.

Viewing Information: The entire region is a haven for woodland wildlife such as white-tailed deer, wild turkeys, birds of prey, forest songbirds, small mammals, and unique reptiles and amphibians. Try rock climbing and rappelling along Big Pine Road, 1 mile east of State Route 374. It's wise to get there early in the day when you are less likely to encounter other climbers. Hocking State Forest is open to hunting during regular hunting seasons.

Directions: *Hocking State Forest Headquarters is located on State Route 374, approximately 4 miles north of South Bloomingville.*

Ownership: DOF (614) 385-4402

Size: 9,267 acres   **Closest Town:** South Bloomingville

**SOUTHEAST OHIO**

60. TAR HOLLOW STATE FOREST

Description: Ohio's third largest state forest is a haven for woodland wildlife. Thousands of acres of steep, wooded ridges of oak and hickory provide habitat for white-tailed deer, gray squirrels, wild turkeys, and forest songbirds. Twenty-two miles of hiking trails lace the northern half of the forest. Thirty-three miles of bridle trails lie south of the fire tower, which gives a beautiful overview of the surrounding forest, especially during fall. Seventeen miles of paved roads and 14 miles of gravel roads offer scenic views as well as ample opportunity to observe wildlife from a vehicle. Tar Hollow is known for its delicious and abundant spring morel mushrooms; a mushroom festival is held each year during April. Tar Hollow State Park also lies within the forest.

Viewing Information: Coey Hollow, in the extreme northwestern section of the forest, has been set aside as a special ruffed grouse management area. A variety of forest animals inhabit this 1,700 acres. From Charleston Pike (County Road 222), take Hough Road (Township Road 262) 1 mile west to Bunn Road (Township Road 261), then north 1 mile to the grouse management area. Tar Hollow State Forest and the Grouse Management Area are open to hunting during regular hunting seasons.

Directions: *From Adelphi, follow State Route 327 approximately 10 miles south.*

Ownership: DOF (614) 887-3879

Size: 16,120 acres　　　**Closest Town:** Adelphi

Timber rattlesnakes, found in the extreme southern part of the state, are an Ohio endangered species. Research into this animal's habitat requirements has been funded by voluntary contributions to the Wildlife Diversity Program, coordinated by the Ohio Division of Wildlife.

61. SCIOTO TRAIL STATE FOREST

Description: Named for the Native American Indian trail that once connected nearby Chillicothe to Portsmouth on the Ohio River, this state forest is primarily mature oak-hickory woodland. White-tailed deer, wild turkeys, gray squirrels, and ruffed grouse are the main game animals. Nongame forest birds include wood warblers during migrations and pileated woodpeckers year-round. The forest surrounds Scioto Trail State Park, offering wetland wildlife viewing at two 15-acre lakes. A fire tower near the forest office gives a good overview of the rugged, hilly terrain.

Viewing Information: If you take a driving tour of the forest, be sure to include South Ridge Road—the views can be spectacular. On foot, try the area around the old airfield along Airport Road and Bethel Hollow. Twenty-six miles of bridle and mountain bike trails, 6 miles of paved roads, and 18 miles of gravel roads provide good access to all areas of the forest. Scioto Trail State Forest is open to hunting during regular hunting seasons.

Directions: *From Chillicothe, follow U.S. Route 23 approximately 9 miles south to State Route 372, then east to the forest office.*

Ownership: DOF (614) 663-2523

Size: 9,390 acres   **Closest Town:** Chillicothe

SOUTHEAST OHIO

A small bird of the deep woods, the ovenbird is named for the domed nests (resembling Dutch ovens) that it builds in leaf litter on the forest floor. Through a small entrance in the side, adults secretly slip in and out of the nest without revealing its location. Cowbirds seem to have little trouble finding the nests, however, as they regularly parasitize them with their eggs. ART WEBER

77

62. COOPER HOLLOW WILDLIFE AREA

Description: Located along the historic Kanawha Trail once used by buffalo, Indians, Colonial militia, and early settlers, this area is primarily reverting woodland wildlife habitat. The extensive oak-hickory forests that once covered the surrounding hills were cut from 1840 to 1890 to fuel more than 40 iron-producing furnaces in southeastern Ohio. The remains of Madison Iron Furnace are near this area's headquarters. White-tailed deer, ruffed grouse, gray squirrel, wild turkey, and waterfowl are the principal species, along with a rich variety of songbirds.

Viewing Information: A trail along the north edge of the swamp near the area entrance is a good place to view wetland wildlife such as wood ducks, mallards, blue-winged teal, painted and snapping turtles, snakes, and frogs. It is also a likely spot to hear the hooting of a barred owl early or late in the day. Other aquatic animals, such as beavers and muskrats, are abundant along Symmes Creek and its tributaries. A woodcock observation area behind the headquarters building is excellent for viewing spring woodcock mating flights at dusk and dawn. Cooper Hollow Wildlife Area is open to hunting during regular hunting seasons.

Directions: *From Oak Hill, follow State Route 279 approximately 0.5 mile east to County Road 2 (CH & D Road), then turn north and go approximately 3.5 miles to the area entrance.*

Ownership: DOW, call 1-800-WILDLIFE for a free area map

Size: 5,420 acres   **Closest Town:** Oak Hill

Bald eagle populations in Ohio reached an all-time low in 1979 with just four nesting pairs of eagles remaining in the state. Since that time, the population has boomed mainly because of the Ohio Division of Wildlife placing captive-bred eaglets into wild nests, a wildlife management technique known as fostering.

63. SHAWNEE STATE FOREST

Description: The largest of Ohio's 20 state forests, Shawnee encompasses more than 60,000 acres and is often referred to as the "Little Smokies of Ohio." Ridge upon ridge of oak-hickory forest provides extensive habitat for woodland wildlife. Wild turkeys, white-tailed deer, ruffed grouse, forest songbirds, small mammals, amphibians, reptiles, and insects are abundant. Fall color and spring wildflower displays can be spectacular. The forest includes Shawnee State Park, with its rustic lodge and cabins. Adjacent Raven Rock State Nature Preserve was once used by Native Americans to scout advancing parties of explorers and settlers on the Scioto and Ohio rivers.

Viewing Information: Shawnee Backpack Trail offers more than 42 miles of walking trails, portions of which wind through 8,000 acres of designated wilderness. For those wanting less stressful viewing opportunities, a drive of the Panoram Loop is a good option. At Picnic Point and other vistas along the route, motorists can see the Ohio River Valley. Use caution driving the narrow, winding forest roads; winter can cause hazardous conditions and road closures. Shawnee State Forest is open to hunting during regular hunting seasons.

Directions: *From Portsmouth, follow State Route 52 approximately 6 miles west to the Forest Headquarters.*

Ownership: DOF (614) 858-6685

Size: 61,648 acres   **Closest Town:** Portsmouth

Known as the "Little Smokies of Ohio," Shawnee State Forest is ridge after rugged ridge of oak-hickory forest habitat along the Ohio River. Woodland wildlife abounds, and scenes such as this golden ragwort growing near a spring stream are common. In addition to wildlife watching at this site, autumn color can be spectacular.
ART WEBER

SOUTHEAST OHIO

79

64. KINCAID FISH HATCHERY

Description: This hatchery raises primarily muskellunge and steelhead trout. Plan a spring or early summer visit, when wildlife viewing is most productive at the 30 outdoor fish ponds. Canada geese, mallards, and wood ducks are common. Plovers, yellowlegs, snipe, killdeer, and other shorebirds are prevalent on the mud flats when the ponds are being drained. Great blue herons and belted kingfishers are common, along with muskrats and beavers in adjacent Kincaid Creek.

Viewing Information: The hatchery buildings are open to the public Monday through Friday, 8 a.m. to 4:30 p.m. The grounds are open dawn to dusk. The hatchery is adjacent to Pike State Forest to the north, where woodland wildlife can be observed. Try Tobacco Barn Hollow in the forest for a hike, or Greenbriar Ridge Road for a driving tour. Pike Lake State Park is nearby.

Directions: *From Waverly, follow U.S. Route 23 south to State Routes 124/32 west, then take State Route 124 12 miles west to the hatchery entrance (approximately 23 miles from Waverly).*

Ownership: DOW, call 1-800-WILDLIFE for a free brochure

Size: 200 acres   **Closest Town:** Latham

Ohio provides an abundance of habitat for aquatic wildlife: 3.25 million acres of Lake Erie, 451 miles of the Ohio River, and 6,000 miles of inland rivers and streams.

80

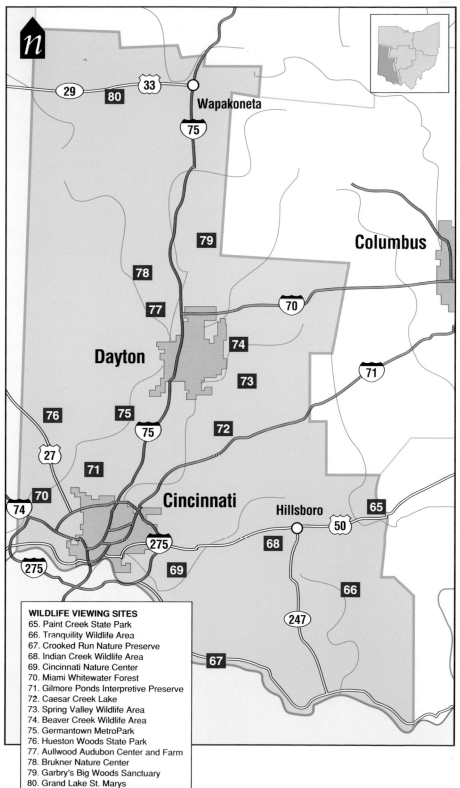

WILDLIFE VIEWING SITES
65. Paint Creek State Park
66. Tranquility Wildlife Area
67. Crooked Run Nature Preserve
68. Indian Creek Wildlife Area
69. Cincinnati Nature Center
70. Miami Whitewater Forest
71. Gilmore Ponds Interpretive Preserve
72. Caesar Creek Lake
73. Spring Valley Wildlife Area
74. Beaver Creek Wildlife Area
75. Germantown MetroPark
76. Hueston Woods State Park
77. Aullwood Audubon Center and Farm
78. Brukner Nature Center
79. Garbry's Big Woods Sanctuary
80. Grand Lake St. Marys

65. PAINT CREEK STATE PARK

Description: This site's primary habitats are grassland, brushland, woodland, and a large lake. Paint Creek Lake provides habitat for waterfowl, shorebirds, and wading birds such as great blue herons. Ospreys and bald eagles have been seen over the lake. Limestone outcroppings along the shore provide nesting habitat for cliff swallows. Songbirds, small mammals, white-tailed deer, and a few wild turkeys inhabit upland areas.

Viewing Information: For upland wildlife viewing, try three areas: near the Pioneer Farm along Deer Park Road; just west of the park office along U.S. Route 50; and north of the camping check-in station along Taylor Road. The lake and its shoreline are visible from many places, such as the overlook near the dam. Eight miles of hiking trails and 25 miles of bridle trails are maintained. Portions of Paint Creek Lake and the adjacent wildlife area are open to hunting during regular hunting seasons.

Directions: *From Bainbridge, follow U.S. Route 50 approximately 5.5 miles west to the park office.*

Ownership: DPR (937) 365-1401

Size: 10,200 acres   **Closest Town:** Bainbridge

Accidentally introduced into this country in 1899 on nursery stock from Europe, the praying mantis now inhabits the eastern United States and southern Ontario. The praying mantis is extremely cannibalistic; the young, which hatch almost simultaneously in spring, are either dispersed by the wind or eaten by one another. Survivors are normally solitary.

JIM ROETZEL

66. TRANQUILITY WILDLIFE AREA

Description: Set in the beautiful, rolling hills of Adams County, this area is a mixture of woodland, brushland, cropland, old field, and small pond wildlife habitats. This area lies just outside the "Edge of Appalachia," where red cedar glades, native grasses, and wildflowers mix with stands of oak-hickory forest. In spring, the beauty of vast numbers of flowering dogwood and redbud trees creates special interest. The headwaters of Little East Fork of Brush Creek are here.

Viewing Information: All of Ohio's typical game species, along with nesting and migrant songbirds, inhabit Tranquility Wildlife Area. Of particular interest are the spring migration of songbirds and the fall migration of hawks. Wild turkeys are common. Tranquility Wildlife Area is open to hunting during regular hunting seasons.

Directions: From Peebles, follow County Road 100 (Old State Route 32) 4.5 miles west.

Ownership: DOW, call 1-800-WILDLIFE for a free area map

Size: 4,200 acres   **Closest Town:** Peebles

67. CROOKED RUN NATURE PRESERVE

Description: This well-managed preserve along the Ohio River has been developed to attract white-tailed deer, wild turkeys, waterfowl, and songbirds. The result is a combination of habitats. Three bird blinds border an estuary, two observation decks overlook the Ohio River, and one observation tower is set in an old field. A 1.5-mile loop trail leads through woods, marsh, field, brush, river, and pond habitat.

Viewing Information: The Ohio River is a natural migration corridor for birds, so this preserve is a convenient resting and feeding stop in spring and fall. Water birds and wetland wildlife are visible along Crooked Run Creek Estuary and the Ohio River. You can see songbirds and upland wildlife around the many food plots and shrubs planted in the area. Beavers are common, and evidence of their tree cuttings is readily apparent.

Directions: From Chilo, follow State Route 222 south to its terminus at the Ohio River, then follow park district signs. A new entrance is planned for 1997 off State Route 52, 0.25 mile east of the intersection of State Routes 52 and 222.

Ownership: Clermont County Park District (513) 732-2977

Size: 77 acres   **Closest Town:** Chilo

SOUTHWEST OHIO

Green darner dragonflies, also known as "snake doctors" or "darning needles," are one of the fastest and largest dragonflies found in Ohio. Adults prey on midges, mosquitoes, caddis flies, and other flying insects. The female inserts her eggs singly into slits cut in the stems of submerged plants. SCOTTY LOVETT

68. INDIAN CREEK WILDLIFE AREA

Description: Nearly 50 ponds, potholes, and shallow marshes distinguish this southwestern Ohio site. Waterfowl, shorebirds, and furbearers frequent these habitats and the narrow valleys of Indian and Little Indian creeks. The remainder of the area is very flat, mainly cropfields and woods mingled with brushland of broomsedge, scattered sassafras, soft maple, pin oak, and gum trees.

Viewing Information: The marsh at the southeastern corner of the intersection of Campbell and Murray Corner roads along the area's northern edge offers good viewing of ducks, geese, coots, herons, kingfishers, raccoons, muskrats, water snakes, turtles, frogs, and dragonflies. Songbirds are abundant throughout the area, and numerous parking lots make easy access for birders. Indian Creek Wildlife Area is open to hunting during regular hunting seasons.

Directions: *From Fayetteville, follow U.S. Route 68 for 1 mile south to Campbell Road, then turn east 0.75 mile to the area.*

Ownership: DOW, call 1-800-WILDLIFE for a free area map

Size: 1,799 acres **Closest Town:** Fayetteville

69. CINCINNATI NATURE CENTER

Description: Cincinnati is the undisputed cardinal capital of the world! The annual Christmas Bird Count reports more Northern cardinals here than anywhere else. Part of that count is conducted on the grounds of the Cincinnati Nature Center, a private, nonprofit, environmental education organization. The center is open to the public on weekdays, but restricted to members and their guests on weekends and holidays. An entrance fee is charged. More than 14 miles of hiking trails wind through woods and fields, along five ponds, a lake, and stream. The nature center building houses a natural history library, displays, classrooms, and a gift shop. Long Branch Farm, a 535-acre interpretive working farm, is in nearby Goshen.

Viewing Information: Hundreds of bluegills and numerous painted, red-eared, and snapping turtles come to the boardwalk on Crosley Lake to be hand-fed by visitors during warmer months. The viewing blind and photography blind offer close observation of birds. Elevated platforms at Fox Rock give a unique view of this glacial outcrop and its unusual plant life such as purple cliffbrake and walking fern.

Directions: *From Interstate 275 east of Cincinnati, take the Hillsboro (U.S. Route 50) exit and follow U.S. Route 50 east approximately 2 miles to Roundbottom Road then turn south. Go 0.6 mile on Roundbottom Road and turn east on Tealtown Road. The entrance to the center is approximately 0.5 mile on the right.*

Ownership: Cincinnati Nature Center (513) 831-1711

Size: 790 acres **Closest Town:** Milford

SOUTHWEST OHIO

70. MIAMI WHITEWATER FOREST

Description: This sprawling area, the largest park in the Hamilton County Park District, consists of streams, wetlands, woodland ponds, an 85-acre lake, meadows, prairie, brushland, young woodland, and old-growth forest. The combination attracts all common Ohio wildlife species. More than 120 acres of wetland have been restored; several hundred acres of tallgrass prairie make this area a unique blend of ecosystems, a boon for native wildlife.

Viewing Information: Trails meander throughout the park. Several offer self-guided nature tours and wildlife viewing. Shaker Trace Trail's two paved, 10-foot-wide, fully accessible loops totaling 8.7 miles take you through diverse habitats. Timberlakes Shelter is the trailhead for three other trails and is also a wildlife viewing blind. The 1-mile Parcours Fitness Trail is easy woodland walking and good birding. The 0.75-mile Oakleaf Trail winds through a stately oak forest and along two woodland ponds where raccoons, mink, white-tailed deer, and an array of birds thrive. Sinkholes and other unusual landforms distinguish the 1.75-mile Badlands Trail. At the southern end of the park, the 0.66-mile-long Tallgrass Prairie Trail leads through forest and prairie. Visit in July or August, height of the bloom, to see numerous bird and butterfly species.

Directions: *From Interstate 74, northwest of Cincinnati, take the Dry Fork Road exit. Park entrances are located off West Road, Harrison Avenue, and Mt. Hope Road.*

Ownership: Hamilton County Park District (513) 521-7275

Size: 3,897 acres   **Closest Town:** Harrison

Ohio's tallgrass prairies are the most limited ecosystem in the state, even more so than wetlands. It is estimated that 1,000 square miles of tallgrass prairie habitat once covered western Ohio, supporting wildlife such as the now extirpated American bison.

71. GILMORE PONDS INTERPRETIVE PRESERVE

Description: This area of southwestern Ohio is a wetland jewel in an urban setting. The old Miami-Erie Canal runs through the preserve; ice cut from the ponds during winter was loaded onto canal boats destined for growing Midwestern cities. More than 230 species of birds have been recorded here, as well as three salamander species, six frog species, five snake species, and seven turtle species. Wetland plants include state-endangered beaked burhead.

Viewing Information: Best viewing is spring and early summer, when ponds and seasonal wetlands are inundated. Bird life abounds; great blue herons, snipes, mourning doves, blue jays, and various sparrows are common. In creeks, watch for muskrats, beavers and their dams. A large butterfly-hummingbird garden near the Gilmore Road parking lot attracts a variety of butterflies. A Butler County Metroparks permit is required for entry.

Directions: *From I-275 north of Cincinnati, take State Route 4 north approximately 3 miles to the State Route 4 Bypass. Follow the State Route 4 Bypass north to Symmes Road, then turn west and go 0.5 mile to the south entrance across from the water tower. The main entrance is located along Gilmore Road to the west.*

Ownership: Metroparks of Butler County (513) 867-5835

Size: 195 acres   **Closest Town:** Hamilton or Fairfield

P S 人 占

A wary, secretive bird of Ohio wetlands, the great blue heron is easily seen because of its large size, but not easily approached. As with viewing most species of wildlife, a good spotting scope or binoculars is recommended for getting close-up views. These birds are colony nesters, and it is not unusual to see 50 to 100 large stick nests in a single heronry.

DONALD M. JONES

SOUTHWEST OHIO

72. CAESAR CREEK LAKE

Description: This large lake and surrounding acreage in southwestern Ohio provide habitat for wetland and upland wildlife. Restored wetlands and prairies attract waterfowl, shorebirds, wading birds, and birds of prey. Caesar Creek Lake is home to gulls, terns, herons, and shorebirds. Pick up trail maps and viewing guides, and acquaint yourself with regional history at the visitor center near the dam. Adjacent to the lake is Caesar Creek State Park, with a public beach and campground. A fossil collecting area is located at the spillway; get a permit from the visitor center.

Viewing Information: The wetland-prairie complex lies along Clarksville Road near the southwestern corner of the lake. Meadows there attract grassland-dependent birds such as grasshopper sparrows, savannah sparrows, and Eastern meadowlarks. Above the spillway, another wetland consists of three small ponds, with a viewing blind available. Portions of Caesar Creek Lake and surrounding lands are open to hunting during regular hunting seasons.

Directions: From Waynesville, follow State Route 73 approximately 2 miles east, then turn south on Clarksville Road for approximately 3 miles.

Ownership: U.S. Army Corps of Engineers (513) 897-1050

Size: 10,550 acres   **Closest Town:** Waynesville

Trumpeter swans, the largest of all North American waterfowl, are now being reintroduced into the state by the Ohio Division of Wildlife after an absence of some 300 years. The goal of the trumpeter swan reintroduction program is eventually to establish a breeding population of at least 15 pairs of swans in Ohio.

73. SPRING VALLEY WILDLIFE AREA

Description: This site was a commercial fur farm in the early 1900s. Today, the habitat highlight is a 150-acre wetland complex harboring a wide variety of wildlife. The remainder of the area is woods, brushland, and cropland. Four miles of the Little Miami River border the area on the west.

Viewing Information: A 2.5-mile trail encircles the marsh, and a boardwalk and viewing tower give good overviews. (The boardwalk is closed during waterfowl hunting season.) Parking areas for the loop trail are along Township Roads 238 and 239. A paved bike path parallels the west side of the marsh near the trail. Ducks, geese, and wading birds are common, as are muskrats, mink, and beaver. Upland habitats provide good opportunity to see and hear songbirds and game birds; more than 230 species have been recorded. Spring Valley is one of the best areas in southwestern Ohio for neotropical warblers. Skunk cabbage and marsh marigold bloom in late winter and early spring in the small swamp west of the bike path. Spring Valley Wildlife Area is open to hunting during regular hunting seasons.

Directions: *From Waynesville, follow State Route 42 approximately 4 miles north to Roxanna-New Burlington Road (County Road 69). Turn east and follow County Road 69 approximately 1.5 miles to the area headquarters.*

Ownership: DOW, call 1-800-WILDLIFE for a free area map

Size: 842 acres   **Closest Town:** Waynesville

One of Ohio's most numerous breeding warblers, the yellow warbler is also one of the most easily identified, by both sight and song. Males are a bright yellow with rusty streaks on the breast. Female colors are more muted. Yellow warblers prefer damp, brushy habitat, such as that found at Spring Valley Wildlife Area. Once a commercial fur farm, Spring Valley is now home to more than 230 species of nesting or migratory birds, as well as a myriad of other wetland wildlife.

GARY MESLAROS

SOUTHWEST OHIO

89

74. BEAVER CREEK WILDLIFE AREA

Description: This unique site contains five of the six wetland types found in Ohio. The most noteworthy is a freshwater fen. The area is unusual in that many of the wildlife and plant species here are common to a more northern climate. Seventy-nine species of breeding birds nest here, and more than 300 species of plants have been recorded, some rare or endangered. Unusual wildflowers include Canada burnet, queen-of-the-prairie, and tuberous Indian plantain. Uncommon animals include bog lemmings, massasauga rattlesnakes, spotted turtles, and sedge wrens.

Viewing Information: A boardwalk made of recycled materials spans the fen and can be reached from the south parking lot along Fairgrounds Road. The fen is a great place to listen for frogs and toads or see migrating wood warblers in spring. Other birds include swamp sparrows, marsh hawks, short-eared owls, and bitterns. The north parking area is located along New Germany-Trebein Road. Beaver Creek Wildlife Area is open to hunting of waterfowl, deer, and furbearers during regular hunting seasons.

Directions: From Interstate 675 east of Dayton, exit at North Fairfield Road (exit 17) and turn south 0.2 miles to New Germany-Trebein Road. Turn east and go 2.2 miles to Beaver Valley Road. Turn south for 2.2 miles to Fairgrounds Road, then east 0.5 mile.

Ownership: DOW (937) 372-9261

Size: 380 acres **Closest Town:** Beavercreek

The largest rodents in North America, beavers were eliminated from Ohio by about 1830. But the population began returning during the mid-20th century. Today there are beaver colonies in every suitable watershed in the state. Other than man, the beaver is perhaps the only mammal able to alter its environment to suit its needs. Look for beaver cuttings and dams throughout Beaver Creek Wildlife Area. Some Ohio beaver dams can be extensive. For example, one dam in northeast Ohio measured 1,200 feet in length. JIM ROETZEL

75. GERMANTOWN METROPARK

Description: Here lies the largest tract of mature forest in Montgomery County, distinguished by a naturally occurring stand of Eastern red cedar trees. Also of interest are a hillside prairie remnant and a spectacular view of Twin Creek from a valley overlook. Observe raccoons, squirrels, opossums, and a wide variety of birds from the underground nature center's viewing window.

Viewing Information: You can see wildlife nearly anywhere along the more than 15 miles of hiking trails. A 500-foot, handicap-accessible boardwalk surrounds the nature center. Broad-winged hawks soar near the prairie. Saw-whet owls hide among cedar branches. Germantown MetroPark is an excellent place to see exposed Ordovician limestone bedrock and fossils.

Directions: *From Germantown, follow State Route 725 approximately 2.5 miles west to Boomershine Road, then turn north 0.75 mile to the entrance.*

Ownership: Five Rivers MetroParks (937) 275-7275

Size: 1,410 acres   **Closest Town:** Germantown

76. HUESTON WOODS STATE PARK

Description: This area of extreme southwestern Ohio contains varied wildlife habitats: mature forest, brushland, open fields, marsh, and open water on adjacent 625-acre Acton Lake. Within the park lies Hueston Woods State Nature Preserve, a National Natural Landmark distinguished by centuries-old beech and sugar maple trees. The nature center also functions as a wildlife rehabilitation facility. Here you can see recovering hawks, owls, bald and golden eagles, and various mammals. An outdoor pen houses white-tailed deer and wild turkeys. Overnight visitors can stay at the rustic lodge or in one of 60 cabins. More than 10 miles of trails attract hikers.

Viewing Information: Find good wildlife viewing at the western edge of Acton Lake. Gulls and great blue herons are common. Mammals include muskrats, mink, beavers, and raccoons. Forest songbirds, along with the big and elusive pileated woodpecker, flourish in the 200-acre "Big Woods" of the state nature preserve. White-tailed deer are common. Note the turkey vulture roost near the lodge.

Directions: *From Oxford, follow State Route 732 approximately 6 miles north and follow the signs.*

Ownership: DPR (513) 523-6347; for lodge and cabin reservations, 1-800-AT-A-PARK

Size: 3,596 acres   **Closest Town:** Oxford

77. AULLWOOD AUDUBON CENTER AND FARM

Description: One of the oldest nature centers in the Midwest, this complex is the Great Lakes regional environmental education facility for the National Audubon Society. The area includes a variety of habitats: woodland, old field, pasture, cropland, marsh, brushland, pond, stream, and a 10-acre tallgrass prairie. Educational aspects include an organic farm and farm animals.

Viewing Information: Numerous hiking trails wind through Aullwood. Not to be missed are views of the prairie from the viewing tower, and the wildlife viewing blind. The nature center includes a gift shop. Aullwood is open year-round, 9 a.m. to 5 p.m. Monday through Saturday; Sunday 1 p.m. to 5 p.m. The facility is closed on some holidays. Admission fee is waived for members of the National Audubon Society and Friends of Aullwood. Pick up a permit to see the 140-acre, planted tallgrass prairie.

Directions: *From Interstate 70 northwest of Dayton, take the State Route 48 exit north 1 mile to U.S. 40, then turn east. Cross the Englewood Dam and turn south on Aullwood Road. The nature center entrance is 0.25 mile on the left.*

Ownership: National Audubon Society and Friends of Aullwood (937) 890-7360

Size: 350 acres   **Closest Town:** Englewood

Of the two fox species found in Ohio, the red fox is more common than its slightly smaller cousin, the gray fox. Reds prefer open country with woodlands interspersed, such as the habitat found at Aullwood Audubon Center and Farm. Grays, on the other hand, mainly inhabit areas of more extensive forest, although both species are found statewide. Males are solitary through late fall and early winter. In January, however, they begin to seek a mate. The pair will take over a woodchuck burrow or sometimes excavate their own den in loose, sandy soil, frequently on the south side of a hill. Most fox pups are born in April. RON AUSTING

78. BRUKNER NATURE CENTER

Description: Besides its long-time role as a nature and environmental education center, Brukner is home to one of Ohio's largest wildlife rehabilitation programs. More than 70 native wild animals, including barn owl, bobcat, and bald eagle, are permanent residents here. Six miles of hiking trails wind through pine forests, deciduous woods, thickets, prairie, and beside swamp, pond, stream, and the Stillwater River. A restored 1804 log house, listed on the National Registry of Historic Places, occupies its original site on the nature center grounds. The interpretive building (nominal admission fee on Sundays) houses hands-on displays, a library, and gift shop. Trails are free and open to the public during daylight hours.

Viewing Information: The glass-enclosed vista room on the third floor of the nature center is intended specifically for watching and listening to birds as they feed. Those who want more active wildlife viewing should hike the Stillwater loop trail paralleling the Stillwater River, or follow the boardwalk that crosses a fen. A viewing platform overlooks the prairie.

Directions: *From Interstate 75 southwest of Troy, follow State Route 55 approximately 2.5 miles west to Horseshoe Bend Road and turn north. The entrance is 2.5 miles on the right.*

Ownership: Brukner Nature Center (937) 698-6493

Size: 165 acres   **Closest Town:** Troy

Project WILD, an award-winning, multidisciplinary school curriculum supplement emphasizing wildlife conservation, is distributed to more than 3,000 Ohio educators annually by the Ohio Division of Wildlife.

Description: The largest tract of old-growth timber remaining in Miami County, this site is a haven for woodland wildlife. Forest songbirds abound in the wet beech-maple forest, and vernal pools provide spring breeding habitat for woodland salamanders and spring peepers. Nesting and migratory songbirds are abundant. Pileated woodpeckers and great blue herons nest here, too. Wildflowers include large-flowered trillium, putty-root orchid, goldenseal, and yellow trout lily.

Viewing Information: A 0.7-mile boardwalk trail loops through the "Big Woods," providing easy access for visitors and protecting sensitive habitats. Nearby but unconnected to the "Big Woods" is Garbry's Reserve. This park is the first place in Ohio to utilize a constructed wetland as sanitary filtration for restrooms.

Directions: *From Interstate 75 at Piqua, follow State Route 36 approximately 5 miles east to Casstown-Sydney Road. Turn south and follow Casstown-Sydney Road to Statler Road, then follow signs to the sanctuary.*

Ownership: Miami County Park District (937) 667-1086

Size: 100 acres   **Closest Town:** Fletcher

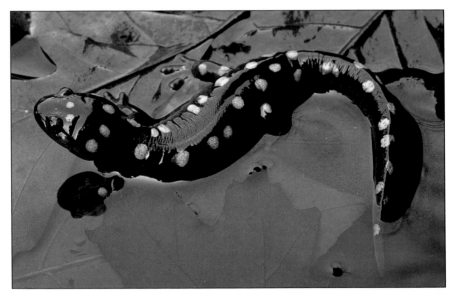

Spotted salamanders are found throughout Ohio in low-lying moist woodlands adjacent to swamps, ponds, and creeks. Because of their secretive nature and their habit of tunneling underground, they are seldom seen except in early spring, when they migrate in large numbers to breeding ponds. Even then they are active only at night.
GARY MESLAROS

80. GRAND LAKE ST. MARYS

Description: At more than 14,000 acres, this is Ohio's largest inland lake. It is a magnet for wildlife, especially birds, in the extreme western part of the state. The lake was built as a water supply for the Miami-Erie Canal and was completed in 1845. Stop to see the canal boat replica in the town of St. Marys on the lake's eastern edge. The towpath along the old canal offers excellent birding. Follow it north or south of town.

Viewing Information: St. Marys Fish Hatchery, along State Route 364 on the eastern end of the lake, is a good place to begin a tour. The hatchery raises mainly saugeye and catfish and is open weekdays 8 a.m. to 4:30 p.m. The 25 outdoor rearing ponds are open to wildlife viewing dawn to dusk and attract a variety of water birds, especially ducks and geese. Mercer Waterfowl Management Area, on the southwestern corner of the lake along State Route 703, is a good place to view waterfowl and grassland birds such as bobolinks and grasshopper sparrows. The refuge itself is off-limits, but substantial numbers of Canada geese are usually visible from the main parking lot. Grand Lake St. Marys State Park has several excellent open-water bird viewing areas: East Bank along State Route 364; West Bank along State Route 703; and Windy Point at the end of Windy Point Road approximately 1 mile north of the town of Montezuma.

Directions: *Grand Lake St. Marys is on the border of Mercer and Auglaize counties between the towns of Celina and St. Marys.*

Ownership: State of Ohio, call 1-800-WILDLIFE for a free area map

Size: 14,362 acres   **Closest Towns:** Celina, St. Marys

For the first time in 150 years, the purple catspaw, an endangered freshwater mussel, was recently found in Killbuck Creek in Coshocton County.

THE WATCHABLE WILDLIFE SERIES
Alaska Wildlife Viewing Guide
Arizona Wildlife Viewing Guide
California Wildlife Viewing Guide
Colorado Wildlife Viewing Guide
Florida Wildlife Viewing Guide
Idaho Wildlife Viewing Guide
Indiana Wildlife Viewing Guide
Iowa Wildlife Viewing Guide
Kentucky Wildlife Viewing Guide
Montana Wildlife Viewing Guide
Nevada Wildlife Viewing Guide
New Mexico Wildlife Viewing Guide
North Carolina Wildlife Viewing Guide
North Dakota Wildlife Viewing Guide
Oregon Wildlife Viewing Guide
Tennessee Wildlife Viewing Guide
Texas Wildlife Viewing Guide
Utah Wildlife Viewing Guide
Vermont Wildlife Viewing Guide
Virginia Wildlife Viewing Guide
Washington Wildlife Viewing Guide
Wisconsin Wildlife Viewing Guide

BIRDER'S GUIDES
Birding Arizona
Birding Minnesota
Birder's Guide to Montana

SCENIC DRIVING GUIDES
Scenic Byways
Scenic Byways II
Back Country Byways
Scenic Driving Arizona
Scenic Driving California
Scenic Driving Colorado
Scenic Driving Georgia
Scenic Driving Montana
Scenic Driving New Mexico
Scenic Driving Oregon
Scenic Driving Texas
Travel Guide to the Lewis & Clark Trail
Traveling the Oregon Trail
Traveler's Guide to the Pony Express Trail

ROCKHOUND'S GUIDES
Rockhounding Arizona
Rockhound's Guide to California
Rockhound's Guide to Colorado
Rockhounding Montana
Rockhound's Guide to New Mexico
Rockhounding Texas

FALCON
1-800-582-2665

P.O. BOX 1718
HELENA, MT 59624